Groups,
Troops,
Clubs, &
Classrooms

Groups, Troops, Clubs, & Classrooms

**THE ESSENTIAL HANDBOOK
FOR WORKING WITH YOUTH**

Susan Ragsdale and Ann Saylor

SEARCH
INSTITUTE
PRESS

Groups, Troops, Clubs & Classrooms:
The Essential Handbook for Working with Youth
by Susan Ragsdale and Ann Saylor
The following are registered trademarks of Search Institute: Search Institute® and Developmental Assets®.

Search Institute
615 First Avenue Northeast, Suite 125
Minneapolis, MN 55413
www.search-institute.org
877-240-7251

ISBN-13: 9781574824889

The following authors and organizations have graciously given permission to the authors to quote and reprint their copyrighted work:

Andrew Newberg, MD, and Mark Walkman, *How God Changes Your Brain*, 2009, Ballantine Books, New York.
John J. Medina, *Brain Rules*, 2013, Pear Press.
Howard Gardner, PhD, *Multiple Intelligence*.
National Dropout Prevention Center, Clemson, SC, www.dropoutprevention.org.
James Vollbracht, *Stopping at Every Lemonade Stand: How to Create a Culture that Cares for Kids*.

Library of Congress Cataloging-in-Publication Data
Ragsdale, Susan.
　　Groups, troops, clubs & classrooms : the essential handbook for youth leaders / Susan Ragsdale and Ann Saylor.
　　　　pages　cm
　　Summary: "This practical handbook is for teachers, volunteers, group leaders, youth counselors, coaches, and anyone with works with young people. Find practical and motivational advice for approaching young people from a strength-based perspective. Readers will learn about how kids' brains are wired, how to create inviting classrooms and meeting spaces, and how to connect with them in meaningful, lasting ways. The authors share dozens of strategies for activating and sustaining young people's innate strengths and skills so they can become positive forces for self-realization and community betterment"— Provided by publisher.
　　ISBN 978-1-57482-488-9 (paperback) — ISBN 1-57482-488-0 (paperback)
　　1. Youth. 2. Youth development. 3. Leadership in children. 4. Community leadership. I. Saylor, Ann. II. Title.
　　HQ796.R235 2014
　　305.235'5—dc23
　　　　　　　　　　　　　　　　　　　　　　　　　　　　　　2014006833

The content of this book has been reviewed by a number of youth development professionals. Every effort has been made to provide sound direction for each activity and method described herein. The authors, publisher, and reviewers take no responsibility for the use or misuse of any materials or methods described in this book, and will not be held liable for any injuries caused by participating in activities and games from this book. Please use prudent judgment and take appropriate safety precautions when participating in all activities and games.

*For all the adults who work tirelessly
to love youth from the inside out—
building their strengths and
helping them discover
how to be their best selves.*

And for the youth who will benefit from your love.

Contents . . . .

PART THREE: Sustaining Power

Foreword . . . .

As I read *Groups, Troops, Clubs, & Classrooms,* I found myself thinking back to the days when I was a graduate student preparing to start student teaching at a large public high school in Boston. That was more than two decades ago, but I still remember the mix of eagerness and nervousness I felt as I imagined standing in front of thirty-two high school juniors every day. I aimed to teach them something useful about American history after the Revolutionary War. To get ready for that challenge, I read and reread the articles about classroom management, and I devoured books on John Adams, the Constitution, and other subjects in the textbook I would be teaching from.

I thought back to those days while reading *Groups, Troops, Clubs, & Classrooms* because this book would have been far more useful than everything I read to get ready to begin my work with kids. Instead of focusing on controlling negative behavior and brushing up on academic content, this book would have introduced me to two big ideas that are even more important. The first is that seeing and building upon *kids' strengths* is far more effective than emphasizing their deficits. The second is that everything begins with *building relationships.*

To some people, those two big ideas—kids' strengths and relationship building—might seem like blinding flashes of the obvious. Certainly, it is easy to grasp their appeal and importance, but it is often hard to put these ideas into practice. That is true not only for classroom teachers, but also for

program leaders, mentors, coaches, and other adults who work with young people in a wide range of capacities.

In this book, Susan Ragsdale and Ann Saylor share a wealth of practical strategies for discovering kids' strengths and building strong relationships. They do that by summarizing complex bodies of relevant research in concise and understandable ways. Most important, they share techniques that they have honed over many years of working with young people in a variety of settings.

When I began reading the book, I decided to circle the games and activities that I could imagine using the next time I need a creative way to engage and energize young people. When I paged back through my copy after finishing the book, I noticed that it was filled with circles and notes in the margins like: "Awesome activity for the first day with kids." There is no question in my mind that my student teaching would have gone better with a bit less John Adams and a few more activities like "Uniquely Me," which you will find on page 105.

While I have no doubt that this book would have been spectacularly useful to me at the start of my work with young people, it was also useful and enjoyable after twenty years of work in education and youth development. Even—perhaps especially—those of us who have been at this for a while need to be reminded that every young person has strengths we can build upon. An old saying goes, *Kids don't care what we know until they know that we care.* Susan Ragsdale and Ann Saylor have created the ultimate guide to showing young people that we care.

Kent Pekel
President and CEO of Search Institute

Introduction . . . .

We've written this book for teachers, youth workers, and other adults work-ing in groups, troops, clubs, and classrooms who want to know *more* about helping young people become the best they can be by drawing from their strengths instead of their weaknesses. If you picked up this book, we know you care about youth, want the best for them, and are looking for ways to engage, enrich, and help them grow in character and wisdom. Perhaps your heart goes out to those who don't quite seem to fit in. Perhaps you delight in seeing the lightbulb go off when they discover something about themselves, "get it," or master a skill. Maybe it's the child who rebels that gets your atten-tion because you understand those impulses. You've been there. Or, maybe you've always had a soft spot for those who are misunderstood by others simply because they are "different" in regard to preferences, intellectual or physical abilities, or ethnicity. If working with youth is part of your life and you want to glean knowledge, wisdom, tips, or even affirmation from these pages, you won't be disappointed.

This handbook is designed to help you create the best experience pos-sible for the youth you're working with. The content is based on a positive, strength-based approach to learning. We provide just enough of the theory and social science behind the strength-based approach to help you under-stand why this philosophy is so important, but mostly you will find stories, ideas, and practical tips for running your program from a strength-based

premise. We have included valuable resources, both here in the book and through online formats, to further help you provide a quality youth program or classroom experience.

A Word about Play

One of the best ways to get to know your group is through play.
In our play we reveal what kind of people we are.

—Ovid, Roman poet

Play is an important tool in our work with young people and adults. We thought it wise to set the stage for its prominent presence in this book and give a little context for this important strategy on the front end.

Nothing creates a safer space for youth to stretch themselves, explore, grow, develop skills, learn, and build relationships than the act of play. A lab for practice, play is an equalizer and a great way for you, the leader, to get to know your youth. In play, you will see personalities and even values come out; you will observe what they enjoy and what they don't; and you'll quickly get to know the individuals in your group. Many times in the space of play, youth can simply "be." Games provide a venue for youth to get away from the real world in a created space and scenario where they can practice new habits, new ways of relating to people, and new problem-solving techniques. It's a place where they can learn.

Take anger management, for example. If youth play with tower blocks and the tower falls, the person who toppled it over might respond with frustration, irritation, or maybe even laughter. With the toppling of the tower, there is a life lesson to be explored about patience and how it takes planning to look for just the right block. Being irrational or impatient creates results you don't want. So, too, is it for life.

Game time is important. We throw the football, talk about video games, or play games. Connect Four, Tumbling Towers, domi-

noes—I use these with all ages. It's a great opportunity to transition from hanging out to talking about something important.
"What does it take to win the game?" becomes "What does it take
to win in life?" Games are like minilives—you just expand them.

—Jake Lawrence, licensed professional counselor

Play is also an opportunity for youth to have fun while practicing skills.
If Susannah is practicing dribbling skills, she can add some fun by practicing
them in relay races with friends before the big game on Saturday. If Lucas is
trying to get comfortable meeting new people, he can practice making eye
contact, shaking hands, and introducing himself in an icebreaker name game
before going to the meet and greet with his congressional representatives.
If Jeremy is learning new strategies for conflict resolution, he can practice
them in a team-building simulation game before he needs to resolve a conflict with a peer.

Play is a powerful strategy for putting into action many of the ideas suggested by research and social science. We know it's worked for us and hope
you will find to your delight that it adds life and energy to your interactions
with youth.

Own the Book

This book is *yours*. Own it fully! We want you to devour it and integrate it
with your thoughts and ideas. That's part of the strength-based experience.
Combine your wisdom and best thinking with our recommendations.

Feel free to mark up the pages of this book. Make notes in the margins about your aha moments and any ideas you want to ponder. Capture
those thoughts in the "Keepers" sections at the end of each chapter. With
a marker or your e-reader's bookmarking and note-taking functions, highlight key activities or concepts that you want to remember. Dog-ear or use
sticky notes to mark favorite pages you want to come back to. Personalize
this handbook so that it becomes a collection of ideas you love.

This book contains reading and video suggestions, quizzes, activities, handouts, and journaling opportunities. We will introduce you to what we call Strategic Moves, or suggestions for how you can put some of the concepts we cover into practice. You'll also find Playful Moves to help you engage young people in active and creative ways. Some chapters contain Take Two writing exercises, where we ask you to take two minutes to reflect on a topic and answer the questions. These exercises are designed to inspire you to think about how you will apply the information you have read about. The goal is always to help you expand power in yourself and your students.

Brain research shows that readers learn more when they interact with a text. When you interact with what you're reading, you will slow down and engage your brain; as a result, you'll be more likely to remember what you read. The more you scan your notes and highlights and the more you write, the more you will integrate what you've learned into your long-term memory. So do the quizzes. Answer the journal questions. Circle answers when asked. The more information you retain, the closer you are to incorporating a strength-based approach into your actions with youth. That's a great reason to make this book yours. In the end, youth will benefit.

PART ONE:
Youth, Strength, and Power

A Strength-Based Approach to Positive Youth Development

Some of you may already know what a strength-based approach is or maybe you are vaguely familiar with the concept. Or maybe this is the first time you have heard the term. Because everything in this book is based on a strength-based approach to positive youth development, let's start out by making sure we're all on the same page. Let's break down the concept of strength-based approach by focusing on its root idea: *strength*.

For many years, we have asked young people and adults about what comes to mind when they hear the word *strength*. We ask how they define it and how they've come to their understanding of strength. We've even asked them to draw pictures to illustrate what strength means to them. Here are a few examples of how people have responded:

Strength is . . .

- Muscles
- The inner ability and power to cope
- I can do this
- Endurance
- Courage
- Patience
- Power
- To be strong in whatever you do

Defining Strengths

How do you define strength? Answer by writing or doodling in the space below.

Strength is . . .

On what do you base your understanding of strength?

Journal Exercise

Pictures frequently include a stick figure of a man gunning his muscles or a picture of barbells—alone or with someone holding them over the head. One memorable picture showed eight different stick figures standing in a circle holding hands, with some of the hands held high in the air. What has become obvious from our queries is that children and youth often talk about strength in a physical sense, whereas more mature teens and adults recognize the importance of inner strength.

The Social Science behind Positive Youth Development

At its core, positive youth development is all about building strengths within youth and providing them with opportunities to be active cocreators of their learning and lives. Our job is to provide opportunities for young people to develop and practice skills, find and pursue interests, and become engaged in community life in meaningful ways. This social science approach is steeped in research and supported over time to be an effective way to help youth grow and thrive. In street lingo, a strength-based approach is *loving kids for who they are and helping them grow from there.*

What do you want for young people? Ask any parent, teacher, youth worker, club leader, or pastor, and you'll hear a desire to raise strong and healthy youth who are confident, joyful, and contribute to the betterment of society. A strength-based approach represents the idea of *at-promise* rather than *at-risk.* It honors the strengths and giftedness innate to youth and strives to emphasize, tease out, and build on the internal and external strengths found within youth's lives. The idea of viewing a child as "at-promise" isn't to paint an unrealistic "pretty" picture; rather, we coach adults to include truths about a child that are left out by the dominant language of being "at-risk," which tends to be negative and even damaging. At-promise broadens the perspective, fills in some of the details, and reminds us that all children have natural gifts, positive qualities, and potential for goodness.

A strength-based approach assumes "what's right" with youth is worthy of our attention way more than "what's wrong." It assumes "what's right" with youth can be found *within* young people and deserves focus and time so that youth become more fully aware of it themselves. As teachers, youth workers, and parents, we *can* help young people grow more fully into capable, thriving human beings.

We wrote the following poem to paint a picture of hope, promise, faith, and potential. The poem asks us to be in young people's corner. We need to root for, believe in, and build on young people's sense of self and dreams to become their very best self.

Believe in Me

Believe in me.
Believe that I have promise for a positive future.
Believe in my strengths and help me grow stronger.
Believe that I can learn from my mistakes and overcome past failures.
Believe that I can make smart choices.
Believe that I can grow and change.
Believe that I can have strong character.
Believe that I can be responsible.
Believe that I can respect myself and others.
Believe that I can resolve conflicts peacefully.
Believe that I can stay away from negative situations.
Believe that I can learn skills for my future.
Believe that I can set and achieve goals.
Believe that I can do well at school.
Believe that I can influence others for good.
Believe that I have gifts to offer.
Believe that I can contribute to the community.
Believe that I can live a life of purpose.
Believe in me.

The poem aptly expresses the underlying tenets of a strength-based approach for youth: intentionality, the teaching and equipping of skills, enhancing abilities, discovering interests, connecting to meaning and purpose, guiding, supporting, providing opportunities for them to contribute and give, and actively engaging them as cocreators of their lives.

Building on Strengths Is Countercultural

Derek Peterson, an international youth advocate, wrote the following advice about working with young people:

> NO . . . person should use the label "at risk." It is meaningless. It is quackery. It drives the mind and the community to ridiculous actions that, too often, further harm kids. I know that we all live in a deficit based culture and are paid to identify and fix problems, repair broken teens, and make dysfunctional families and communities work. However, what asset based thinking brings to the conversation is that 1) everybody has things that are RIGHT about them, 2) we can fix a problem by approaching the solution through our strengths and competencies, 3) we can't repair a broken teen, but we can show him/her resilience, and have them understand that we have all been broken at one time or another, and we'll probably become broken again—life is difficult, and 4) we can't make anyone do anything. All we can do is enter their circle, support others in seeing the world through different eyes, provide the tools and knowledge to move toward their identified goal and way of being, and then work alongside them to make it all happen . . . CELEBRATING and LAUGHING all the way, while constantly rewarding RELATIVE BEST.

The act of focusing on strengths is different from the cultural norm of zoning in on what needs "fixing." The danger of a "fixing" mentality is that you can unknowingly create a gap between you and those you love. The tendency is to see youth as lesser than yourself.

A strength-based approach calls for seeing youth as whole and in light of their capabilities, strengths, and possibilities. So instead of approaching youth with the idea that you are going to fix them somehow, look closely for their strengths. Instead of focusing on "what's wrong" with a child, look within him or her to find talents, gifts, and inner resources to draw out. You start with what is right, good, and strong within and about them and use those innate gifts to foster positive growth. You emphasize the positive.

Here is another insight from Derek Peterson on how to approach young people:

> I have found that, for the most part, I live *in to* the stories that people tell me about. If those who have influence upon me believed in me, and communicated those positive expectations, and gave me opportunities to practice and grow into those expectations, and finally celebrated my "relative best" attempts, then, for the most part I lived into those expectations.

We believe in the best of youth. Always. And that belief shows up and plays out in what we say and do on a consistent basis. And we *work* from strengths rather than from deficits. We *work* to help youth realize their potential and to gain a healthy sense of self. We *work* to set expectations of them and of ourselves to live into our own innate goodness.

Positive youth development is steeped in a belief that youth have value now, not just when they become adults. Youth have important things to say about culture, education, and decisions. They have unique perspectives and can contribute to solving today's problems, so it's important to strive to engage them in the conversation. Your role is to provide opportunities for youth to give back, work side by side with others, and have roles that are meaningful and impactful. You offer supportive relationships and guidance.

The Vision You Hold

Take some time to reflect on the following questions:

What do I really want for my youth?
What qualities do I hope they develop and internalize?
What opportunities, people, or experiences do I see in their lives?
What hopes do I have for their futures?

Close your eyes, think about these questions, and then jot down some of your thoughts below.

Journal Exercise

I Believe! I Believe! Now What?

A strength-based approach to youth work is vital for unlocking potential and nurturing goodness within each young person. Those who operate from a strength-based approach carry a certain mind-set of core beliefs about the rights of youth:

- Every young person, despite deficits or challenges, has strengths, resources, and gifts, even if obscured. They have the right to discover those strengths and who they are.
- Youth are capable and competent. They have the responsibility and the right to give of themselves to others and to make a difference.
- Youth need the transformational power of hope. When youth believe there is hope for a better future, they are able to envision, face, and strive for that future. They have the right to dream big, aspire to greatness, and have meaningful opportunities.
- Youth need safe places to grow and explore. They have the right to be safe.
- Every youth needs to be surrounded by caring adults who provide support and opportunities to encourage the young person's growth. They have the right to have adults who believe in them and tell them so. Repeatedly.

Those who are able to say yes to these core beliefs exercise a final, unswerving commitment. They never abandon a faith in the inner power, giftedness, and greatness of young people. They look for even the minutest indicator of greatness as confirmation. They listen to the dreams of youth, encourage them, expect greatness, believe in them, vocalize that belief, and continuously call forth the strengths youth have within themselves. They actively work to help youth realize their potential, recognize it, and live fully from it.

EXERCISE

Assess Yourself . . . .

Now it's time to do a quick assessment. Read the statements below and note how well you currently do in focusing on young people's strengths and accentuating their positive qualities. Using a scale of 1–10 with 1 representing "I don't do this at all" and 10 representing "I do this extremely well," write the appropriate number after each statement. Be honest. Most of us fall short in some areas. This assessment is for your eyes only. It is not a means for beating yourself up or putting yourself on a pedestal. It's meant to give you a clearer picture of how well you see yourself carrying out the desires you listed in the journal section of this chapter—the ways you want to see youth treated. After you assess, go back and identify one or two actions you want to use more often to improve your impact with youth.

I can name individual strengths in each of the youth with whom I engage.	
I make it a daily practice to acknowledge others' contributions, skills, and gifts.	
I help youth identify and name their strengths and abilities.	
During conflict, I point out what they are doing well and help them identify strengths that can help them resolve the conflict.	
I make an effort to have one-on-one check-ins with each youth in my program or classroom.	
When dealing with difficult situations, I make sure I voice sincere encouragement and affirm my belief in young people.	
I ask young people about what matters to them.	
I ask young people their opinions on all sorts of subjects that are meaningful and real.	

I intentionally provide opportunities for youth to lead activities.	
I intentionally act on young people's ideas.	
I encourage youth to set life goals.	
I counter negative self-comments I hear from youth by getting them to state a positive about themselves.	
I listen closely to their ideas and don't dismiss what they have to say.	
I provide opportunities for youth to practice and use their power to make things better.	

FOR YOUR BOOKSHELF

What Kids Need to Succeed: Proven, Practical Ways to Raise Good Kids, by Peter L. Benson, Judy Galbraith and Pamela Espeland (Free Spirit Publishing, 1998).

All Kids Are Our Kids: What Communities Must Do to Raise Caring and Responsible Children and Adolescents, second edition, by Peter L. Benson (Jossey-Bass, 2006).

Putting Positive Youth Development to Work

Employing a strength-based approach in your program will take some practice, but, thanks to educators who went before you, you have some solid tools to rely on. Search Institute's Developmental Assets® framework is the godfather of positive youth development. The assets are frequently referred to as "building blocks," an apt description that brings to mind an image of laying a foundation upon which something solid and lasting is built. The blocks, or assets, are individual and community strengths that support healthy development over the life of a child. The beauty of these building blocks is that they are backed by more than 25 years of research.

The asset list is comprised of 40 commonsense qualities that have a powerful influence on the life of a child beyond Maslow's hierarchy of needs. These qualities have been tested with over three million young people across the United States. Research bears out that the more assets present in a young person's life, the greater his or her chance of leading a meaningful life. When a young person has many assets, his or her strengths, capacities, and resources increase to the point where he or she makes good life choices and exhibits thriving actions, such as volunteering, leading, maintaining good health, and succeeding in school. Likewise, participation in unwise actions decreases. Youth with high numbers of assets are less likely to engage in risky behaviors such as violence or drug or alcohol abuse. To learn more about how assets impact youth development, you can visit www.search-institute.org to dig into Search Institute's research or to access the age-specific lists.

Asset Categories: The Broad View

Let's take a wide-angle view of the eight broad categories of assets to get a feel for these strength builders.

Support: Surrounding youth with people who love, care for, appreciate, and accept them.

Empowerment: Involving and empowering youth; giving away power.

Boundaries and Expectations: Setting understandable guidelines on what behaviors are acceptable or not, with encouragement and challenge for youth to be their best self.

Constructive Use of Time: Involving youth in positive, healthy activities in programs and at home that reflect their interests.

Commitment to Learning: Supporting and helping develop a strong interest in, and commitment to, education and learning (about all sorts of things).

Positive Values: Developing strong values that guide choices.

Social Competencies: Supporting youth in acquiring and expanding skills that help them make positive choices, build relationships, and deal with difficult situations.

Positive Identity: Developing a strong sense of power, purpose, worth, and promise.

Each of these categories gives clues to what is needed for young people to become caring and competent. They describe the environment, relationships, and qualities youth need from those around them. Some assets reflect things you can have a direct influence on (your role) while others connect more to the internal hard drive of a young person that he or she must embrace, adopt, and put into practice. In the latter cases, you can speak to those assets, encourage them, and create opportunities to tease them out, but at the end of the day, youth must choose for themselves whether to live them out.

How the Assets Work

We want you to look at these broad asset categories in a very direct and personal way. Think of a specific young person you care about and want to influence in a positive way. Perhaps it's a family member, a neighbor, a student, a program participant, or someone from your place of worship. Think of one child you want to see succeed.

Now think about the strengths you see in this young person. What are they? Think about the various skills and talents that he or she has. What are the attitudes and values within this person that shine? Do you notice certain activities that this young person loves to do or is good at? What resources do you see in this young person's life (people who care or opportunities available)? Who is there to encourage, listen to, and support this young person?

For example:

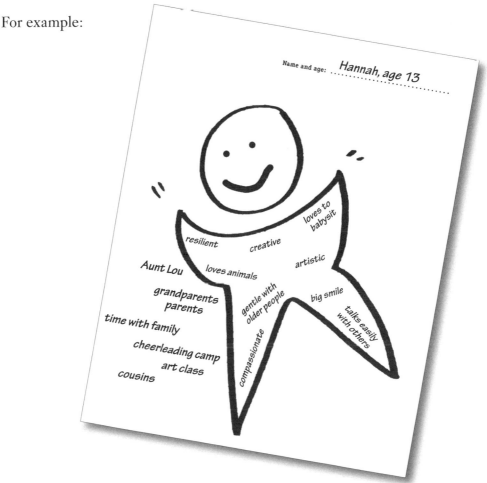

Step two is identifying one to three concerns you have with the young person. Step three of this exercise requires looking at the asset categories and comparing them to the strengths you see in your young person. Can you connect the dots between what you see in your person and the assets? If you see a direct match or "it's in the same ballpark," note it by writing the asset next to the listed strength. If you don't see a match, leave it blank. This exercise gives you a simple example of what assets look like in the real world.

For example:

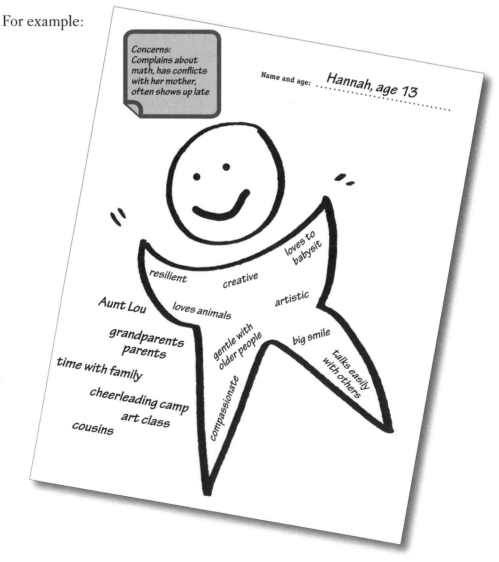

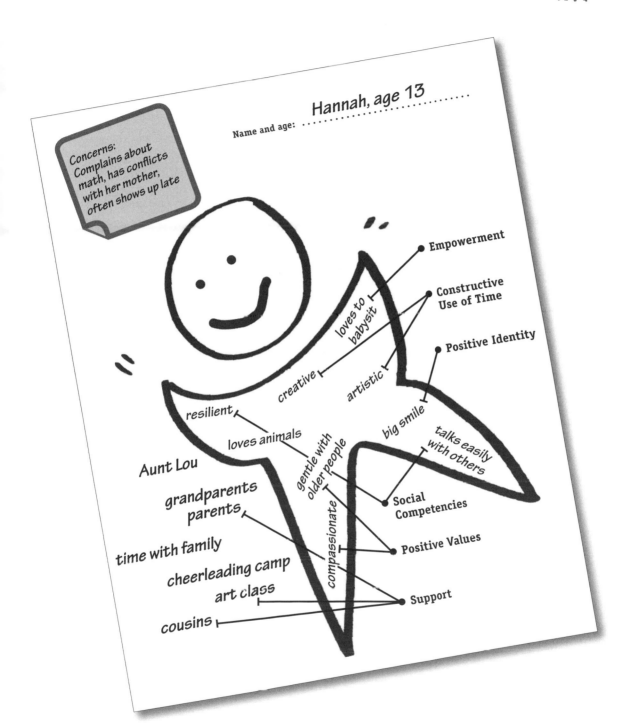

EXERCISE

Your Star Person. . . . .

Now it's your turn to focus on a specific young person. Draw your star person, listing the young person's strengths, passions, values, winning attitudes, and resources. Then think about your concerns and list them. Remember to include the assets when you make notes about this young person.

Name and age: . . . .

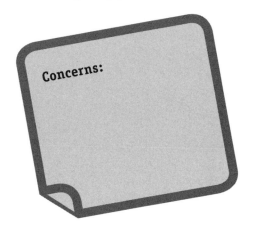

Concerns:

Exploring Your Program

Now, apply this strength-based research to your program. Think about your program and what your youth gain or learn from it. What strengths are you building? What capacities are you enhancing? What values or attitudes are you influencing? What concerns are you addressing? Picture your classroom or program as a car wash. When you take your car through the car wash, you know it will look different upon your exit. When young people leave your program, you want them to be different too. You want to be able to say that they have grown in the knowledge, skills, or support that match with your program's or classroom's core values. What will youth have when they leave your classroom or program?

Going back to our example, when Hannah goes through our art leadership and service program ("our car wash"), we want her and others to gain the following qualities or knowledge:

1. How to help meet community needs
2. How she can use artistic abilities to serve community needs
3. A sense of confidence in her own power to make a difference
4. An increased sense of compassion and empathy

EXERCISE

Your Turn . . . .

List three to four strengths you want to build or concerns you are trying to address in your classroom or program.

1.

2.

3.

4.

Star the strengths or concerns that you directly influence or emphasize in your program that match a specific asset or category. Write the asset name next to it.

Example:

Art Leadership and Service Program

1. How to help meet community needs *

Empowerment

2. Use artistic abilities to serve community needs *

Constructive Use of Time

3. A sense of confidence in her own power to make a difference

Positive Identity

4. An increased sense of compassion and empathy

Positive Values

· ·

This Your Turn exercise illustrates that youth have strengths that you can influence, and they have strengths that are developed elsewhere. It shows, too, that you can't address everything; after all, your program isn't designed to be the only positive influence in a life. However, by partnering with others you can increase your influence to address concerns and to build strengths. It's a village effort, and the assets give you the language to talk about and focus on what is needed.

Congratulations! You have just identified various ways that you are already using a strength-based approach within your work and life. By connecting the dots between what you do and the Developmental Assets, you have solidified your work with respected, trustworthy research, and you have identified best practices to help youth succeed and be their best.

If, for some reason, you found that your dots were *just a little* short of connecting, don't worry. Simply use the assets as a guide to adjust your efforts and focus your work further until your actions and activities align with the best practices in assets.

EXERCISE

How Did I Do? . . . .

Do a gut check and circle the number for each statement that fits how you're feeling.

1. I impact assets and never even knew it.
2. I have been impacting assets more by who I am and how I show up than by any deliberate plan.
3. My classroom or program impacts assets that fit perfectly with our goals. It's a match.
4. My classroom or program impacts assets, but we could be more deliberate in how we go about it.
5. I have a lot of work to do, but I am encouraged.

EXERCISE

Assets in Action Match . . . .

Use this review activity to help you solidify your knowledge and get the hang of identifying assets in action in the real world. Match the action on the left with the appropriate asset on the right by drawing lines. Note that some assets will have more than one action. The answers to this exercise are at the end of this chapter on page 28.

1. Julie knows and can name eight neighbors in the neighborhood.	Support
2. Miranda takes art classes after school.	Empowerment
3. Quesi says he rarely gets bored during school.	Boundaries and Expectations
4. Sosha delivered food to people without power after a big storm.	Constructive Use of Time
5. Ricky returned money when he realized he got too much change from the cashier.	Commitment to Learning
6. Melanie loves to plan big events.	Positive Values
7. Leon thanks young people when she sees them taking on leadership.	Social Competencies
8. Gentry is in the middle of a good book.	Positive Identity
9. Mr. Jones encourages each student to give his or her very best.	
10. Marcella can't think of anyone else she'd rather be. She's happy being herself.	

TAKE **TWO** After reading and thinking about the Developmental Assets, what do you want to remember? What makes the assets different from other youth development theories or your own experiences? How do you think implementing assets in a deliberate way could improve your program? What could you do?

. . . .

The Pull of Power

If you want youth to realize the vast multitude of resources and strengths within themselves, you must provide opportunities for them to access and utilize their own power, which translates into sharing some of your power. Achieving this demands an attitude check on the part of leaders. It requires that you occasionally examine your attitudes, beliefs, and prejudices. It compels you to learn to put your faith in youth into practice in concrete and tangible ways. And sometimes it tests you and challenges you to break free from childhood programming or to break free from "adultisms" and egos.

The idea of power has cultural overtones. In the United States, adults are often taught to claim power, and youth learn to defer power. To build strengths in youth, you will need to redistribute the balance of power. You must share power, and you must help youth access power. And when you do this, you become more powerful. In a practical sense, the act of sharing power is the application of working from a strength-based approach. It moves the needle from discovery of strengths to acting on them.

Suggesting that you share power with youth might create some intense reactions: "Give away power? I can't do that. I'm responsible for what happens in the program." Or, "I'm held accountable for my classroom." Other adults may say, "Give away power? I tried that. And just as I thought, the youth really didn't want it. They said they did, but they didn't do anything with the opportunities." The desire—whether it is unconscious or based on a lack of trust in youth leadership or even a fear of what will happen if you give your power away—to hold on to your power is a natural response. It may appear easier to keep your power. We, however, have found that power isn't an either-or situation. Sharing power is really about creating *more* power.

When power gets into the peer space, it starts to expand. It causes other youth to say things such as, "How come I didn't get to lead the icebreakers today?" It creates a demand for opportunity and power. Think of it as a new equation in which $2 + 2 = 5$. Sharing power doesn't take away from what you can do; rather, it increases what each person can do. When youth take charge of things in the classroom or program that they can do well, then the adult is freed up to focus on other matters.

Strategies for Expanding Power

To expand power effectively, you need to develop leadership in youth, and this requires some strategy. Having a concrete plan may help you "let go" of your old idea of power more easily as you begin to share and expand power with youth.

Start small. Begin to notice the everyday moments when youth defer power to you when they could easily hold on to it themselves and change the power flow. For example, if a young person comes to you and asks for a definition of a word, hold back and refrain from giving him the answer. Ask him where he could find the answer for himself. In this simple moment, you have asked him to think, recognize he has the power to find the answer, and realize his own sufficiency. He can claim, in a small way, his own power. And, for you, it begins to generate a discipline of sharing power, giving back to your youth what they can do for themselves.

Think through the little tasks and what youth can already do. What do they already have the skills, know-how, and resources to pull off? What goes into making your classroom or program work? Do you have snacks? Play music? Use icebreakers? If your youth can research a subject online, order snacks, kick off meetings, or lead icebreakers, then why are you doing it? Surely, children can help choose music or lay out snacks. Surely, teens can lead icebreakers. As they assume these responsibilities, you can do something else. As youth get more experience, they gain a stronger sense of ownership and skills, and you will be able to do more as a group. When you successfully share power, you can do more with your time (personally and as a group) and you expand the power. You create a space of shared interests and tip the cultural idea of claiming and deferring power to one that says, "You're more powerful now and so am I."

Identify where young people need training and then train them. As an adult, you are accountable for the processes in your program and for what you teach. If an opportunity comes up for a young person to speak before a business group, you can't just say "go for it" and expect great results. Instead, you help that young person prepare for public speaking. Likewise, you can help a child find an icebreaker or prepare to lead a discussion. You will also need to guide the young person in accepting the accountability side of sharing and expanding power. Part of sharing power is preparing young people to be ready to take on their newfound power. Some tasks or jobs simply require training, and it's up to you to provide it.

Training can be time consuming, and how a young person completes a task will not look like how you do it. That's okay. But over time, the results of your efforts will be multiplied because of your team leadership approach. You will get more done, and you will have a bigger impact on the youth than if you maintained the cultural norm to claim and keep all power for yourself.

Trust the Process

The goal is to get to the point where you can trust that, as you share and expand power, youth will step up and take on the tasks and responsibilities. Be warned that this won't happen overnight. They won't take you up on it instantly. Just as you've been taught to claim power, they've been taught to defer. They are in the habit of deferring to adults. Sharing power successfully may take months because youth need to trust that you really mean to do what you say. Sometimes they've been asked for their opinions, only to have them minimized. Sometimes they've been asked to take leadership roles, only to be marginalized or have the power withdrawn when they make a faulty decision. Usually young people's decision-making responsibility is snatched by well-meaning adults. Youth want power, but they need to know that you are serious about power sharing. They need to believe it and *see* it, and they need to practice what it feels like to have power. Remember, they probably haven't *seen* what a 14-year-old with power looks like and most likely are not even sure how to use power appropriately.

Power sharing takes time, trust, and continuous effort. Remember to start small by inviting youth to take on little tasks. Check in with them frequently, always communicating your faith in their ability to do the job well. Continuously express the new message of power; don't let young people's deferral of power stay a habit in your space. Change the message and the reality. Be patient with how long it takes. Keep asking for their opinions, input, and leadership. Respond with respect when you get it. Celebrate their attempts, their successes, and their growth. As they prove their reliability and discipline, give them more responsibilities and more power to lead.

Finally, keep watch. Observe the expansion of power. Watch how you are able to create more power and expand the power within the group as a whole. Watch as it begins to layer and as youth become models for their peers on leading with power. Watch and be proud. You can become a dynamic builder of power in others.

Searching Within

How do you expand power to young people on a weekly basis?

What keeps you from giving them more power?

How could you start the process of expanding power with one or two young people this week?

How has sharing power expanded the power in your group? How has it made you more powerful? How has it made others more powerful?

Journal Exercise

Assets in Action Match Answer Key

1. Support
2. Constructive Use of Time
3. Commitment to Learning
4. Positive Values
5. Positive Values

6. Social Competencies
7. Empowerment
8. Commitment to Learning
9. Boundaries and Expectations
10. Positive Identity

 Keepers. . . . .

What do you want to remember from this chapter? What might you use or try? Flip back through the chapter and skim for possibilities or keepers. Record the ideas that intrigue you, seem possible, or make you excited.

. . . .

FOR YOUR BOOKSHELF

Take It Personally: Valuable Insights for People Who Care about Kids, by Jolene Roehlkepartain (Search Institute Press, 2009).

The Best of Building Assets Together: Favorite Group Activities That Help Youth Succeed, by Jolene L. Roehlkepartain (Search Institute Press, 2008).

Hidden Treasures of Assets Game (Grades 3–12 English), a board game by Kelly Curtis and Wayne Whitwam (Research Press, 2008).

Understanding How Young People Are Wired

One of the most fascinating aspects of working with children and youth is marveling at what they come up with. Wait. That might be one of the most trying aspects of working with them! We know from simply watching television commercials that young people's brains aren't fully developed until their mid-20s. We know this, but living with it and responding to it on a daily basis is a different matter altogether.

The past few decades have produced a wealth of knowledge on the marvelous mystery that is our brain. Every year scientists discover more and more about how the brain works, functions, and thrives. These findings offer insights into the drives that wire us as humans, as well as facts on the conditions the brain needs to thrive. This chapter notes some of the factors that are most pertinent to helping shape positive youth experiences; these are factors that teachers and youth leaders can consider and influence.

Brain Needs and Brain Enhancers

We've combined the research of brain scientists with our experience to create a list of 13 distinct influencers that contribute to the healthy development of the brain. We call these influences "brain enhancers" and hope these strategies will help you establish practices that maximize your impact on youth.

Get Moving

In his book *Brain Rules*, John Medina shares 12 known facts about how the brain works and what we can do with that information. One of these known facts is that movement is a brain enhancer. Exercise helps get the blood pumping, increases oxygen, and as a result increases the capacity to learn. The increase in oxygen caused by movement helps people become sharper mentally. Movement helps people pay closer attention and increases focus. Exercise is proven to reduce stress and aid in retained learning.

STRATEGIC

MOVES

- *Build movement into your classroom or program routine: stretching, marching in place, playing charades or games, dance breaks, running laps.*
- *Kick off meetings with a short game or a five- to ten-minute walk.*
- *Incorporate movement into the meeting even in small ways: stand instead of sit to discuss ideas; answer questions by walking to one side of the room or the other to "vote with their feet."*

Games to Encourage Movement

The Walk and Talk strategy from our book *Get Things Going*: Give pairs of students a focused conversation topic, which they discuss while walking. After the walk, they report two discussion points to the rest of the group.

Follow the Leader: Youth take turns calling out a physical exercise move for everyone to do.

The Alphabet Action Game: Divide into groups of three to eight players. When you call out a letter, each team must think of an action that begins with the same letter and simultaneously perform the action. For example, if you call for a "C" action, one group might crawl around. Another group might clap their hands. The first group to simultaneously perform an action wins a point. The team with the most points at the end of game time wins.

Include Novelty and Exploration

One of the great things about being young is that there are lots of "new" things in life: new experiences, new exposures, new things to learn. The brain responds well to new circumstances. Change signals the brain to be alert and pay attention because something important or exciting might happen. Additionally, youth have a natural curiosity and fearlessness. Exploration is in their nature, and Medina talks about the importance of giving our brains time to explore new things. Novelty and exploration work well together, so take advantage of the natural inclinations of this age group.

STRATEGIC

MOVES

- *Change activities every 10–15 minutes.*
- *Change methods and styles frequently. (See page 47 where multiple intelligences are discussed and page 122 where sparks are discussed.)*
- *Encourage young people to try something new: activities, classes, friendship circles, and clubs.*
- *Find out what your young people really like to do.*
- *Offer a variety of activities that invite youth to try different things.*
- *Build in opportunities for youth to explore and become familiar with their community, community problems, and how they can help.*

Challenge the Brain

Has anyone ever told you that you are stuck in your ways? Challenge is the answer to linear thinking. Provide problems and scenarios that call for the brain to look at things from different angles. Randomness maximizes the brain's ability to make multiple connections and associations. Linking new information with previous information or experiences expands the brain's capacities. Although the brain likes challenge, keep in mind that youth who have not been challenged might at first resist trying something that seems difficult.

STRATEGIC

MOVES

- *Assign memory exercises and puzzles (crossword, jigsaw, story, who-done-it).*
- *Pitch complex problems for youth to grapple with and challenge them to brainstorm or to solve the problems quickly.*
- *Use both sides of the brain by combining words with pictures (see "Games to Challenge Youth"). The left side of the brain involves speech (and writing), while the right side of the brain involves drawing and is where meaning is processed.*

Brain Developers at Work

Fourth-grade teacher Linda Tupper of Columbia, Tennessee, is deliberate when it comes to preparing her youth for standardized testing. She knows that her students will be sitting for a great length of time and need all the brain support they can get. While she can't control the length of time they have to spend taking the tests each day, she does what she can to boost brainpower and help them recover as quickly as they can. She focuses on creating a supportive environment before, during, between, and after test taking. She has water and healthy snacks on hand, plays music, leads planned exercise breaks, and has puzzles and coloring pages set up around the room. Linda knows how important healthy development is, and over the years her youth have earned some of the highest standardized scores in the school.

Games to Challenge Youth

Draw-off from *Great Group Games for Kids*: Give teams of four to six youth paper and a pen. Call out a letter and ask players to draw pictures using the letter as a base. For example, the letter "B" turned sideways might become part of a pair of glasses, the eyes on an owl, scales on a monster's back, or even wide-legged pants. Have the teams draw as many pictures as they can imagine in two minutes. When time is up, have teams show one of their pictures.

Use any strategy-based games you have on hand: Risk, chess, checkers, solitaire, Ticket to Ride, Catan, mahjong.

Talk to One Another

Not texting, not using chat features, but talking face-to-face or over the phone. Honest to goodness, real conversations. Having real conversations with others is one of the best ways to "use your words" and not lose your language skills. When you don't use your words, the brain does not function as well. Most of the time conversations involve, by nature, two or more people. Dialogue calls for us to interact with others. That interaction is an important function in keeping our cognitive abilities healthy according to Andrew Newberg, MD, and Mark Robert Waldman, authors of *How God Changes Your Brain: Breakthrough Findings from a Leading Neuroscientist.* If we stay isolated, on the other hand, our ability to interact declines and even mechanisms in our brains may be damaged. Thus conversations are important not just for language but for larger impacts, such as cooperation and maintaining a healthy brain. The more you go deep, get philosophical, think about answers, and feed into two-way, "real" conversations, the more you engage your brain. In addition, you develop and practice valuable communication skills.

STRATEGIC MOVES

- *Keep a bag of questions and let small groups draw out a question to answer together. Use silly questions ("What lollipop flavor would you like to create?") or deeper questions ("What is one way you would like to make a difference in the world?").*
- *Use the 30-second Spotlight Activity from our book* Get Things Going. *Set the timer for 30 seconds and give each person 30 seconds to talk on a topic. This encourages the quiet folks to speak up, while also keeping your ramblers from talking endlessly.*
- *Incorporate time in your program for youth to really talk with each other about things that matter to them.*

Smile, Laugh, and Develop a Sense of Humor

Newberg and Waldman note that smiling is one way to help the brain stay healthy. Even if faked, a smile can disrupt a foul mood, boost your mood, and improve the mood of others. When you smile at others, they tend to respond in kind and the muscles in the faces and bodies of those who are smiling tend to relax. The simple act of smiling actually aids the brain's ability to maintain a positive outlook.

Have you ever heard that laughter is good for you? The old adage is true: "All work and no play makes Jack a dull boy." Laughter increases oxygen flow to the brain, releases endorphins (the brain's feel-good chemicals), and decreases stress. This promising practice is something to keep in mind as you run your program or class; not only does it aid brain health but it also improves moods and lightens spirits. Laughter eases tensions and builds relationships, making your work enjoyable. Enjoy your youth and let them enjoy you. Find ways to laugh together.

STRATEGIC

MOVES

- *Challenge your youth to take a day to smile at others and keep a journal with notes about how they feel and about how others react.*
- *Make memorization fun by turning the work into a game.*
- *Share clean, fun YouTube videos or taped comedians.*
- *Turn on some music and start singing.*
- *Incorporate crazy props, voices, and costumes into skits and presentations to ignite laughter.*
- *Use funny comics or cartoons to start educational presentations.*
- *Consider including tasteful jokes, cartoons, and games in your program.*

A Game to Encourage Laughter

Ha-Ha from *Great Group Games on the Go*: To get things
started, have one player lie down on his or her back.
The next player lies down with his or her head on the
first person's belly. Players continue lying down in this fashion
until everyone is connected head to belly. Without actually laughing, the first player says, "Ha!" the second, "Ha! Ha!" the third,
"Ha! Ha! Ha!" and so on, each player adding an additional "Ha!"
If someone laughs for real (and it's bound to happen), the group
must restart the game with a new leader starting the laughter.

Incorporate Music

In the world of brain development, it appears that music can harmonize brain
rhythms, helping to energize, focus, or calm us. When used effectively, certain genres, such as classical music, can help brains retain information and
enhance learning. Fun, upbeat music can help energize students or create a
good feeling in your classroom or program. Music can be used during fun
times or at the end of programs.

STRATEGIC

MOVES

- *Find all kinds of free music from websites such as Pandora
  or Songza.*
- *Use music to regather the group, to transition between activities,
  or during breaks.*
- *Play classical or soft music during moments when young people
  are doing quiet work.*

A Game to Bring Music into Your Program

Song Off from *Great Group Games on the Go*: Hands down, this is our favorite musical game. Split the group into four teams and have them stand in different corners of the room or play area. Explain that you'll give teams the same word, such as *love,* and they'll have one minute to compile a list of songs that include that word. Once time is up, tell them you'll point to each team, one at a time, to sing a song line within three seconds using the word you gave out. Announce that you're the song judge or recruit others if you aren't confident in your musical knowledge. A group is out if they repeat another group's song, make up one on the spot, or don't sing within three seconds. Start the singing and let the fun begin!

Take Time for Meditation

Meditation is the practice of quieting down and being still, usually through regulated breathing; focused attention on a particular goal, feeling, or word; the maintenance of a relaxed posture and state of awareness; and enhanced mindfulness. Research shows that meditation enhances physical and emotional health. It allows our thoughts to be less chaotic and more connected to our emotions, life, others—to everything.

Newberg and Waldman's research proves that meditation can help change brain pathways and enhance brain functions. In one of the researchers' groups, participants who meditated only 12 minutes a day for 8 weeks showed improvements in cognitive skills. They were able to alter the normal function of their brains. The group specifically enhanced memory recall, concentration, and verbal fluency. These results indicate that the practice of meditation is worth sharing with young people, who can benefit from strategies for relaxation, focus, memory retention, and learning to control emotions in times of conflict. Newberg and Waldman shared that research supports the use of meditation techniques with youth to improve academic performance through "decreased test anxiety, nervousness, self-doubt, and concentration loss," as well as impacting "absenteeism, school rule infractions, and suspension days." And, as can be expected, youth reported an increased sense of well-being and in one study even showed improvement in spatial memory.

STRATEGIC

MOVES

- *Explore how to incorporate meditation into your youth program.*
- *Do a Google search on free meditation guides, music, and breathing exercises on YouTube.*
- *Even a five-minute meditation at the beginning of class can make a positive difference for individuals and in the overall group energy. And youth might choose to adopt this practice in their personal lives.*

Make Time for Feedback and Reflection

Feedback is a form of reflection and response. It might take the form of conversation, a note, an expression, a correction, a suggestion, or a question to help the person think more deeply about an issue. Feedback is essential. It helps us connect with the world and understand our connection to others. Reflection and feedback help us evaluate learning and apply new knowledge. Providing opportunities for regular constructive reflection and feedback supports growth in classrooms and programs. These opportunities will also help youth develop skills for evaluating their emotions and thoughts as well as for giving and receiving feedback. These are skills that will prepare them for life and the work world.

STRATEGIC MOVES

- *Provide opportunities for youth to interpret or share new skills and information they have learned in your class or program.*
- *Use skits, plays, poems, role plays, conversations, and written checklists or feedback surveys to demonstrate what young people are learning.*
- *Allow youth to give feedback to each other (depending on what you are doing).*

A Game to Encourage Feedback

Tiny Teach from *Great Group Games*: This game allows youth to teach and demonstrate what they've learned. Set up by pairing up youth and noting that all players are resources and have something to share with others. Give each pair five minutes to teach each other something, such as counting to five in a foreign language, shooting the perfect free throw, cooking a certain recipe, or folding a paper airplane. Tell youth that you will be asking for volunteers to share what they've learned when time is up. Allow extra time if needed. Ask for volunteers to demonstrate or describe what they learned. Note the variety of skills that were learned about the group and how everyone had something to share.

Little Einsteins, Little Professors from *Great Group Games for Kids*: If you are concerned that some students may not be able to think of something they know well enough to teach, give them some topical areas to help prompt their thinking. In the game Little Einsteins, Little Professors, we offer four topics for young people to choose from: sports, the kitchen, games, and school. This activity is great for emphasizing power sharing, because it demonstrates that young people and adults both have something to offer and teach each other. Pair youth and adults together. Have the youth teach the adult first. Reverse roles. Continue instructions.

Reduce Stress

According to Medina, stressed brains are distracted and retain less information than calm brains can. When under duress, the thinking brain (the cerebrum) literally shuts down and the fight-or-flight (survival) mode kicks in. Stress, it should be noted, is not confined to major life traumas. Even minor incidents such as temperature (the room is too cold or too hot), hunger pangs, lack of sleep, uncomfortable seating, body aches (including growth spurts), insecurity, and fear can stress the body. Anything that causes discomfort can create stress. When stressed, the brain is distracted from thinking and learning.

While you can't control how much stress youth undergo outside of your program, you can use some simple tactics to minimize stress when they are with you. Have water and snacks available to curb thirst and hunger. Monitor the room temperature. Play music to help youth transition to a new setting or activity. Play calm classical music to help soothe students or play upbeat music to energize them. Establish group boundaries so everyone knows the rules, what to expect, and what happens if a rule is violated. Help young people find ways to de-stress. Help them learn how to work through feelings. Find ways to laugh, exercise, stretch, write, talk, or give expression through art.

STRATEGIC

MOVES

- *Be mindful of environmental stressors and do what you can to alleviate them.*
- *Teach breathing techniques for relaxation.*
- *Listen to and be there for youth.*

Drink Water and Lots of It!

Brain tissue is comprised of 80 percent water. For optimal function, it is important to stay hydrated. Water is an essential nutrient and so often overlooked. Inexpensive, water is a must for keeping bodies and brains functioning and thriving.

Using Movement to Counter Stress

Jake Lawrence, a licensed professional counselor who works with children and adolescents, starts some of his sessions with some good old imaginative play. He especially enjoys "sword play," a kickback from his youth. Jake encourages his student to imagine the scenario (battle) he finds himself in and to create a story about it. Then, the two of them battle with foam noodles, letting off steam by yelling and laughing and "sword" fighting. It helps him connect with each student on an individual basis, provides a safe space to de-stress and laugh, and offers both challenge and novelty (creating the story, being a knight). Then they can chat about what's going on in the real world.

STRATEGIC

MOVES

- *Make sure water is easily accessible and encourage youth to drink it.*
- *Enhance water with fresh lemons or limes.*
- *Avoid sugary drinks, which initially increase energy and then cause a drop in energy.*

Practice Focusing and Keeping Attention

Medina shares how the brain needs to be actively engaged in order for us to fully pay attention. It's not possible to multitask when you really need to pay attention to something that requires a high level of concentration. Say you're giving a mini-lecture and your youth are listening while also multitasking. While you're talking away, perhaps they are texting someone, playing a video game, or posting on Facebook. Multitasking with the technology in hand (which has become so common in our society) is merely a digital distraction that takes youth away from what you are teaching. When working with youth, it is important that you create hands-on learning experiences to hold their attention and keep them—and their brains—active.

Craft your activity so that they have to be fully present and engaged: drawing, moving, working, and so forth.

- *Mix up what you're doing every 10–15 minutes. After 10 minutes, attention begins to drop and wander unless you do something emotionally relevant or something that captures their attention.*
- *The brain likes patterns so connect new ideas to things they already know about. Connect the dots between patterns.*

Feed Short- and Long-Term Memory

Have you ever wondered why you have to constantly parrot information to your group even after you've said it countless times? It all has to do with memory. Medina talks a lot about the relationship between our brains and our memory. The brain can only hold about seven factoids of information for 30 seconds. Your youth need to repeat that information to remember it. If they don't, it disappears. If they do repeat it within 30 seconds, their brains can hold it for up to one to two hours. If they don't repeat it again, it will go away. If we want our youth to really know something, we need to get them to repeat it and use it. In our work with youth, our role is often to teach: academics, character lessons, or 21st-century skills. And we want those lessons to stick. Repetition is a necessary act to help youth take in and remember key points. You have to "'peat and repeat" to move ideas and information into short- and then eventually long-term memory. The more they practice and repeat the lesson, the more it sticks.

- *Know your key points and communicate them clearly.*
- *Teach only one to three concepts at once; the brain can only retain a few new concepts at a time.*
- *In the morning, have youth say out loud a new word and its definition. Ask them to repeat it again in the afternoon. The next morning, ask them to use the word in a sentence.*
- *The key is to have your youth repeat to remember. Repeat to remember. Repeat to remember.*

Yawn and Yawn Often

Yawn. We all do it. Often when tired or bored. We tend to apologize if we do it in front of others. Perhaps because we think it's rude or maybe because we realize how contagious it is. However, believe it or not, yawning is actually good for you. So good, Newberg and Waldman recommended that you do it often. Yawning helps release stress and tension. And it is beneficial for helping regulate the metabolism of the brain. The aftereffect is immediate—yawn and you are instantly more fully present, alert, and relaxed. Deliberate yawning quickly brings you to a heightened state of awareness. Try yawning several times. Note how many yawns you have to do before you feel not just relaxed but alert and fully present. This easy brain supporter is one you can do at any time you need to—and it's free!

- *Ask your group to yawn five to ten times before big tests, big performances, or sporting events and during and after tense moments.*

Brain Power

We talked about 13 brain enhancers:

1. Get Moving
2. Include Novelty and Exploration
3. Challenge the Brain
4. Talk to One Another
5. Smile, Laugh, and Develop a Sense of Humor
6. Incorporate Music
7. Take Time for Meditation
8. Make Time for Feedback and Reflection
9. Reduce Stress
10. Drink Water and Lots of It!
11. Practice Focusing and Keeping Attention
12. Feed Short- and Long-Term Memory
13. Yawn and Yawn Often

Ponder the list of brain enhancers and record three that you want to use to strengthen your program. For each enhancer, list one or two ways you can employ it. Keep in mind that if challenge, novelty, and feedback are good for our young people's brains, the same holds true for us. Stretch yourself. Make sure that one of your ideas is new and different from what you've tried in the past.

1.

2.

3.

Journal Exercise

Be patient with yourself as you try new strategies. If you try something different and it doesn't go well, that's okay. You were trying something new, remember? We don't expect our young people to be perfect, so why should we expect that of ourselves?

Keepers . . . .

What do you want to remember from this chapter? What might you use or try? Flip back through the chapter and skim for possibilities or keepers. Record the ideas that intrigue you, seem possible, or make you excited.

. . . .

FOR YOUR BOOKSHELF

Brain Rules: 12 Principles for Surviving and Thriving at Work, Home, and School, second edition, by John Medina (Pear Press, 2014).

How God Changes Your Brain: Breakthrough Findings from a Leading Neuroscientist, by Andrew Newberg and Mark Robert Waldman (Ballantine Books, 2010).

Why Do They Act That Way? A Survival Guide for the Adolescent Brain for You and Your Teen, reissue edition, by David Walsh, PhD (Atria Books, 2014).

How Youth Learn: Ned's GR8 8. YouTube. www.youtube.com/watch?v=p_BskcX TqpM&feature=youtu.be.

Transcendental Meditation in a New England High School. YouTube. www.youtube.com/watch?v=Yni1REJYK6E.

How Young People Think and See the World

Teenagers are people. Children are people. Each young person is an individual with specific interests, skills, attitudes, capacities, needs, desires, and dreams. Each youth sees and thinks about the world and his or her place in it differently, based in part on how the brain is wired. In this chapter we want to explore how very, very smart and uniquely crafted our brains are.

When we think about the major influences on our understanding of how youth are wired, we think of Howard Gardner, a developmental psychologist and author of *Frames of Mind: The Theory of Multiple Intelligences.* Gardner made a name for himself within the educational arena with his research and work on a singular idea. He proposed that when it comes to processing information and problem solving, individuals do so in multiple ways instead of relying on one and the same way (which is what IQ tests are designed to measure). His resulting theory of multiple intelligences (MIs) recognizes that none of us thinks and processes in exactly the same way but that we tap into several different ways to process information and solve problems.

Gardner identified eight intelligences that had to meet a range of criteria, starting off with the "the ability to solve problems." How we express our intelligence depends on various factors, including genetics, experiences, and what our culture emphasizes as important. (To learn more, read his papers at www.howardgardner.com/multiple-intelligences/.) These capacities can be combined in numerous ways to make up our intelligence, but we usually have one or two qualities that dominant how we learn. You, for example, may problem solve and think best (or dominantly) when ideas are presented in a group setting. Cherie may do her best problem solving when she has the opportunity to be more quiet and introspective. Tim may do his best thinking when he gets to use numbers and work through the problem logically. And Sharon might do her best thinking while she's pacing, walking, or even on a jog.

If each of us possesses a unique blend of MIs to draw from, and our mix is completely individual and related to how we are wired, how do you succeed in teaching a roomful of youth?

In this chapter we introduce the eight MIs and provide ideas for how you can better connect with youth as you begin to look for clues to their unique wiring. To get started, we want you to think about your experiences and observations on what you know about how youth *learn*. Take a moment to check in with yourself on your observations of how youth engage with the world.

Learning Styles . . . .

How much do you know about how youth learn and retain knowledge? Quiz yourself on what you know. Select the best choice from each pair of statements below.

1. a. Youth learn best by school-style lectures.
   b. Youth learn best through varied, experiential learning.

2. a. Youth learn best with visuals.
   b. Youth learn best by multiple sensory experiences.

3. a. Youth retain the most through a combination of visual and auditory clues.
   b. Youth retain the most when they get to practice and teach others.

· ·

If you leaned toward the "B" answers in the Learning Styles quiz, you are already aware that humans learn best in situations where multiple senses are engaged in diverse ways. When we teach youth, we need to vary our methods to capitalize on the learning styles of different people because we all learn a little bit differently.

Gardner's work around MIs has had a lasting impact on education. By questioning the idea of intelligence being a singular entity easily measured by a simple IQ test, his MI theory invited us to think about how much broader, deeper, and richer our capacities are.

The core intelligences are as follows:

Linguistic/Verbal (word smart—written or verbal)
Logical/Mathematical (numbers/reasoning smart)
Spatial/Visual (picture smart)
Bodily/Kinesthetic (body smart)
Musical (rhythm/music smart)
Interpersonal (people smart)
Intrapersonal (self smart)
Naturalist (nature smart)

Within your group or class, you may have seven or more multiple intelligences (MIs) staring back at you as you prepare to lead an activity. All those MIs will be combined in a variety of ways, making each young person unique. To effectively connect with everyone in your group, you will have to use numerous approaches and angles to deliver whatever content you are trying to get across. In short, your students are smart in multiple ways and learn best when their particular types of intelligences are engaged. So the burden is on you to follow this formula: Vary your methods. Increase your reach. Increase your impact.

It's that simple.

Vary Your Methods

If you want to make a key point stick with young people, you have to present the concept in multiple ways. If you never vary your method, your message may fall flat, reaching only a fraction of your youth. If Josie's primary MI is movement oriented, then sitting in a seat for an hour will not engage her because her "body smarts" make her antsy to move or create something while she learns. To learn, she needs to be able to work hands on or to move. Another student, Leo, may be primarily "picture smart" and need visuals to help him remember key concepts. Reach them both by using multiple techniques that match their smarts.

Keep in mind that each person has a full *range* of intellectual capacities. A student may have one or two primary dominating styles for learning but also be fully capable of accessing more styles. For example, take ballerinas. Performing requires them to access their "smarts" in body, music, spatial, and even interpersonal intelligences as they try to create a relationship with the audience and weave their story through dance. A smart leader or teacher varies his or her instructional methods in order to reach young people in the ways they learn best. Those methods might be through connections to nature, music, quiet time, or movement. By varying your methods, you reach more youth. In addition, you as well as your youth can start to identify how they think best and managing your group tends to become easier.

Using Multiple Intelligences in Your Program

While there is no scientifically approved assessment that measures a person's particular MIs, we have included a quiz we adapted from the National Dropout Prevention Center that will help you get a general idea of your particular style. Once you have identified your own primary MI, you can assess how you use MIs in your programming.

Assessing My Multiple Intelligences . . . . QUIZ 9

Complete each sentence below by filling in the blanks with the number that best indicates your degree of expertise. Total the score for each intelligence in the box at the bottom of the section. Circle your top two MIs.

4 — Exceptional Expertise   **3** — High Expertise
2 — Moderate Expertise   **1** — Minimal Expertise   **0** — No Expertise

Linguistic/Verbal	I read and understand what I've read with	
	I listen to the radio, CDs, and recorded books with	
	I play word games, like Scrabble, with	
	I make up tongue twisters, nonsense rhymes, or puns with	
	I use words in writing or speaking with	
	In my English, social studies, and history courses in school, I displayed	
	Others have recognized that my writing shows	
	I often convince others to agree with me with	
	I speak in public with	
	I use words to create mental pictures with	
	TOTAL	
Logical/Mathematical	I compute numbers in my head with	
	In my math and/or science courses, I displayed	
	I play games or solve brainteasers that require logical thinking with	
	I identify regularities or logical sequences in things with	
	I think in clear, abstract concepts with	
	I find logical flows in things that people say and do with	
	I categorize and analyze information with	
	I piece together patterns from separate pieces of information with	
	I use symbols to manipulate data with	
	Others have recognized that my deductive ability shows	
	TOTAL	

Spatial/Visual	I am able to use color with	
	I use a camera or camcorder to record what I see around me with	
	I do jigsaw puzzles, mazes, and other visual puzzles with	
	I format and lay out publications with	
	I find my way around unfamiliar territory with	
	I draw or paint with	
	In geometry classes, I displayed	
	I understand what a shape will look like when viewing it from directly above with	
	I design interior or exterior spaces with	
	I recognize shapes regardless of the angle from which I view them with	
	TOTAL	
Bodily/Kinesthetic	I play tennis, golf, swim, or engage in some similar physical activity with	
	I sew, weave, or engage in some similar creative activity with	
	I build models, do woodworking, or construct things with	
	In activities or courses requiring physical or manual dexterity in school, I display	
	I use gestures or other forms of body language to convey ideas with	
	My physical coordination displays	
	I dance with	
	I express my feelings through physical activity with	
	I am recognized as having physical or manual abilities that exhibit	
	My dramatic ability shows	
	TOTAL	

Musical	I sing with	
	I can tell when a musical note is off-key with	
	I can sight read and sing or play a difficult musical piece with	
	I can hear a melody once and reproduce it with	
	I reproduce or create intricate rhythms with	
	I create new musical compositions with	
	I am recognized by others as having musical talent with	
	I direct others in creating musical selections with	
	I "hear" the patterns within a musical piece with	
	I play an instrument with	
	TOTAL	
Interpersonal	I provide advice or counsel to others with	
	My ability to facilitate group work shows	
	I make friends with	
	I play social games such as Pictionary or Charades with	
	When teaching another person or groups of people, I display	
	In leading others, I exhibit	
	My involvement in social activities connected with my work, church, or community displays	
	I am able to understand the needs and emotions of others with	
	I work together with others to achieve a common goal with	
	I sense other people's motives or hidden agendas with	
	TOTAL	

Intrapersonal/Introspective	I reflect on ideas or events with	
	I achieve personal growth by using new information with	
	I achieve a resilience to setbacks with	
	I have developed a special hobby or interest with	
	I set important goals for my life with	
	I use feedback from others to recognize my strengths and weaknesses with	
	I use solitude to strengthen my inner resources with	
	I am strong willed or independent minded to a degree that exhibits	
	I keep a personal diary or journal to record the events of my inner life in a way that displays	
	I seek to understand my own motivation with	
	TOTAL	
Naturalist	I can see variations in leaf patterns with	
	I can identify a wide variety of insects, birds, or rocks with	
	I read scientific and/or nature articles with	
	I can be outdoors and enjoy Mother Nature with	
	When taking a walk, l look at trees, flowers, birds, and the nature around me with	
	I am able to identify stars, planets, and galaxies with	
	I can plan and plant a garden with	
	I like and am able to work with all types of animals with	
	I can watch the clouds and/or identify them with	
	In science classes, I displayed	
	TOTAL	

Adapted and used with permission from the National Dropout Prevention Center, www.dropoutprevention.org.

Multiple Intelligences and Managing Behaviors

Seven-year-old Taylor was constantly interrupting group time by getting out of his chair or speaking out of turn. When he was given play dough to hold and massage (body smarts) during group, he suddenly became focused. Tapping into Taylor's style benefited the entire group.

Multiple Intelligences and Your Youth

When you engage young people, what MIs do you use most often? For example, do you find yourself always teaching through music and rhymes? Do you make it a priority to include learning games in your programming? Do you try to find opportunities to include nature in your group time? Use the space below to describe any correlation you notice between your primary MIs and the way you most often engage young people.

Likewise, what MIs do you notice in your youth? Have you noticed a child losing all track of time while reading? Does another young person tend to use lots of body movement (hands gesturing, use of neck and head, shrugging of shoulders, etc.) when she is talking? Does he pore over Sudoku and logic puzzles? These are potential indicators of MIs.

MIs don't need to be secret ammunition that only youth leaders are privy to. Helping youth discover their MIs gives them new information to consider about themselves. This newfound self-knowledge and awareness can help them navigate more successfully in new situations. It can also be useful in considering study strategies and career choices.

STRATEGIC

MOVES

- *Consider giving the MI quiz to your youth.*
- *Watch and listen to youth with the intention of determining their MIs.*

Connecting with Students

We have repeatedly discovered the truth of this equation: *Vary the methods. Increase your reach. Increase your impact.* Here's a story Susan tells about the process of discovering one student's connection point:

> I was leading team building for a leadership group. In preparing the activities, I checked them against the eight MIs to make sure that I wasn't doing the same style all day long. I wanted to give every opportunity possible for each student to shine and light up with delight at least once over what was happening in the day. In addition, the teacher had singled out a few students she wanted me to draw out or focus on for one reason or another. One girl in particular had been very quiet in her classes and had yet to emerge out of her shell. She was a puzzle.
>
> I kept an eye on her as the morning started, and she didn't seem engaged. All of that changed when I challenged teams to create boats out of straws that needed to float and hold a water bottle. Suddenly, the normally quiet student was a dynamo in charge of her group, animated and leading. Her logic and visual smarts came into play as she worked to solve the problem. The teacher saw this girl's MI style come to the forefront for the very first time and now had something she could work with. She had clues for what worked to pull out leadership within this student.

Strengthening Intellectual Capacities in Youth Programs

Engaging youth through an MI that is not your own strength can be challenging. It takes intentionality, and it takes practice. Here's your chance to try. We've included two ideas for reaching each type of MI, but we want you to personalize your approach. Think about your group and write another two to three strategies for each MI you could use to engage youth. Draw from your experience, web resources, ideas from our recommended books, and ideas from your colleagues.

EXERCISE

Using Multiple Intelligences to Foster Learning and Growth

MI Type	Fostering "Smarts" in Your Program	Your Ideas
1. Interpersonal Intelligence (People Smart)	• Involve youth in group activities, presentations, and projects. • Ask youth to give you a "temperature check" on the group's mood or understanding of a topic.	
2. Intrapersonal Intelligence (Self Smart)	• Encourage youth to set goals to further develop their skills. • Use personality quizzes to help youth discover more about what makes them tick.	
3. Logical/ Mathematical Intelligence (Numbers/ Reasoning Smart)	• When things go wrong, help youth think through what they could do differently next time. • Include logic scenarios/problems in programming activities.	
4. Linguistic/ Verbal Intelligence (Word Smart)	• Ask youth what they're reading. • Use role plays, poems, or lyrics to support program activities.	
5. Spatial/Visual Intelligence (Picture Smart)	• Ask youth to show you their artwork or blueprints. Recruit them to design websites, brochures, program newsletters, or blogs. • Ask youth to create visuals as a way to problem solve or think through given scenarios.	
6. Musical Intelligence (Music/Rhythm Smart)	• Talk about music. Ask youth about their favorite songs and share yours. • Use different kinds of music to engage youth during breaks, quiet reflection time, or in activities. Let them create songs around learning points or themes.	

MI Type	Fostering "Smarts" in Your Program	Your Ideas
7. Bodily/ Kinesthetic Intelligence (Body Smart)	• Use charades as an activity to communicate a key program point. • Let youth stand and stretch *during* activities.	
8. Naturalist (Nature Smart)	• Incorporate thoughts about nature into activities (e.g., a poem on trees). • Take your program outside.	

A Game to Connect Smarts

PLAYFUL MOVES

True/False Scramble: It takes practice to focus on connecting to multiple intelligences. Here's an example of how we connect "body smarts" with "math smarts." Have your group divide into two relay teams and line up. Show them a big ball and a smaller ball. The big ball represents True and the smaller ball represents False. Read out loud an age-appropriate math statement such as 2 + 2 = 5 and then push both balls. The two people at the head of each line scramble to get the right answer. In this case, they would be scrambling to get the smaller ball (because the statement was false) and to bring it back to you (or a student you've chosen to be facilitator).

EXERCISE

Super-Duper Double Your Smarts Challenge! . . . . . .

Pick two numbers between one and eight. Look at the chart "Using Multiple Intelligences to Foster Learning and Growth" to find your two numbers. Write down the corresponding intelligences here:

1.

2.

Set a timer and take five minutes to design a relationship-building activity that emphasizes the two styles you chose. Ready? Set? Go!

Activity name:

Activity:

How does the activity include each MI?

Initial Thoughts

How might varying your teaching methods to include various MIs impact student learning?

What is one MI strength you tend to leave out? Why?

What is one MI you need to be more intentional about including (based on your group)? (You can answer this one after you determine the various smarts within your group.)

Journal Exercise

Merging Multiple Intelligences into the Strength-Based Game Plan

So the tricky part is combining what you know about how the brain works and multiple intelligences, what you've learned about a strength-based approach and incorporating it into your daily schedule. Add on top of that the curriculum you're trying to teach or the skill you're trying to build, and my goodness! Where does the time go?

We realize that each program is different and has certain curricular requirements that have to happen. Nevertheless, try to organize your agenda so that it is sensitive to how youth are wired, what they need, and how they learn. Make sure that your lesson plan includes a relationship plan or developmental plan, if you will. Following is a generic structure of what a daily strength-building schedule for an after-school setting might look like:

10 minutes: relationship check-in and time to explore various stations

This encourages youth to decompress and transition from the school day. It's a prime opportunity to build the Support assets. It's a great time to include novelty and youth choice.

5 minutes: icebreakers and movement

This is a great opportunity to use exercise, novelty, movement, and games to awaken the brain, increase bonds within the team, and introduce the topic of the day.

20 minutes: brain time/creativity

Curriculum time might include planning, homework, creating, serving, or learning. Remember to involve youth in the planning/presentation where possible and to vary presentation by MI styles and in consideration of brain needs for novelty and exploration and to keep their attention by using puzzles, drama, videos, conversations, writing, art, or objects to prove points. Invite guest speakers to bring in different perspectives and teaching styles. This time frame will heavily emphasize the Commitment to Learning and Constructive Use of Time assets.

15 minutes: skill building

Practice, develop, and demonstrate skills for the sake of personal development. Remember to use MIs and brain techniques to enhance youths' reception of the material: consider using games, creativity, and reflection. As you are building technical or academic skills, remember that you are also building social, cultural, and leadership skills at the same time.

10 minutes: closing

Vary closings to include free time or a variety of reflection activities, encouraging individual youth choice and skill building. End well. This is a great time to focus on the assets of Support and Positive Values and to close sessions so that youth know they are a priority to you. Relationships are what keep them coming back!

This schedule is just an example of how you could think about the flow of your program or class. Your main priority is to plan your curriculum according to your young people's developmental needs and your strength-based goals.

· ·

 What would you like to intentionally include in your group time to make sure you tap into multiple strength-based strategies (multiple intelligences, brain development, giving youth power)?

-

-

-

· ·

A Final Word about Youth, Strength, and Power

James Vollbracht, author of *Stopping at Every Lemonade Stand: How to Create a Culture That Cares for Kids*, gives this wonderful advice:

> We must remember that children are very new to the world and don't have the sense of context that we do. Everything they see, hear and experience becomes a part of them. We are stewards of this most important resource, to which we have unquestionable responsibilities: to shield them from harmful and inappropriate experiences, to provide them with opportunities and invitations to participate in the life of the community that will allow their innate gifts to unfold naturally, to guide them through important rites of passage, and to love them unconditionally.

Throughout this section, we've reflected on strength and power, and we've explored how each young person is uniquely wired. We've discussed brain research and MIs. We've also provided strategies and ideas to help maximize your programming efforts. By building on the strengths naturally found *within* young people, you can draw them out and support them to be their very best selves.

What we hope you get out of this section is to be mindful of the experience that you create in your program or classroom. The way you interact and the way you engage become part of who your students are. What you do shapes them. Knowing how your young people are wired and being intentional about what you do is one aspect of positive youth development. Seek to build on their strengths and work *with* young people according to how they are wired. Working *with* can make all the difference.

Keepers. . . . .

What do you want to remember from this chapter? What might you use or try? Flip back through the chapter and skim for possibilities or keepers. Record the ideas that intrigue you, seem possible, or make you excited.

. . . .

FOR YOUR BOOKSHELF

Multiple Intelligences: New Horizons in Theory and Practice, revised and updated, by Howard E. Gardner (Basic Books, 2006).

"What Is Your Learning Style?" Edutopia, www.edutopia.org/ multiple-intelligences-learning-styles-quiz.

"Multiple Intelligences Worksheets," Statewide Parent Advocacy Network, www.spannj.org/rasicrights/appendix_b.htm.

PART TWO:
Activating Power

Preparation: The Work before the Work

In part 2 we move into concrete ways you can put positive youth development into action—from how you approach and set up space to the actions you take to connect with and get to know youth to the strategies you employ to engage, stretch, and challenge them. This section of the book is all about activating youth power and putting their strengths and gifts into action.

We start by teaching you how to prepare, including being mindful of how you create the space to make your program safe, inviting, and full of opportunities for them to have a say in what happens.

The Prep Work

Being prepared for a group means having a plan A, B, C, and sometimes D—at least in your head. For example, you had planned activities for 45 youth but only 10 show up. You were supposed to have a guest speaker, but she suddenly cancels. Now what? How can you make the time together meaningful and worthwhile? Or, you planned for two hours of programming or instruction, but circumstances beyond your control interrupt your plan. Now you now have 45 minutes to get across a meaty subject like dealing with bullies, learning the secrets of closing a debate, reducing fractions, or planning a service project. What do you do?

Here's what we've learned:

Try not to take yourself too seriously. Relax and be willing to adapt your plan. Keep the flow moving so that the time you do have with them *is* meaningful.

Have more games, activities, examples, and ideas than you will use. If you are overprepared, you will have the flexibility to add, delete, or move content as needed.

Have a variety of ways to approach your content. When 10 people show up instead of 45 (or vice versa), you can adapt your methods. This strategy also means being able to present content in different ways to accommodate various learning styles. Consider the multiple intelligences in your group when developing each lesson plan. Challenge yourself to use at least two or three styles so that you are engaging as many youth as you can in what you do. Mix it up. Present information visually, verbally, with movement, and so forth.

Have flexibility in the content. Sometimes you come in ready to get across a key message or explore a subject only to discover that your group isn't where you thought they were. Let go. Meet them where they are. That might mean taking a deeper dive into your topic or introducing the idea and slowly beginning to work on it. Sometimes you have to swim in the shallow end of the discovery pool.

Be willing to let go. On occasion, you might have to totally adjust your plan. Be present enough to know when forging ahead with an agenda is useless because the young people in your classroom or group are not "there." And if they aren't there, they aren't going to receive your message, and they won't see you as the person who is truly present for them. Have a plan but be ready to adjust to the circumstances. Be flexible and adaptable, read the group, and adjust as necessary. It's an art!

Besides having a game plan that incorporates these aspects, there is one more step in preparation that needs to be addressed before (and then during and even after) you engage with youth. It has to do with your attitude. If you recall, in chapter 1 we talked about your mind-set and positive youth development. We want to say a little more here.

We suggest that you adopt an attitude and expectation of what our counseling friend Jake calls "unconditional positive regard" that you will maintain no matter what. Unconditional positive regard is a belief that no matter what happens or what is seen, this person (the youth in front of you) is *good* even if he or she has done terrible things. Even if the good isn't obvious. Everyone has the capacity to do good. Your job is to believe that and offer encouragement to your group to cultivate it.

This is the attitude you commit to *before* you meet any child, *during* your interactions with your youth, and even *after* those trying moments when they walk away and you want to start grumbling and generalizing about "kids today." It's okay to get the frustrations out of your system, but always return to center: to a belief and hope in unconditional positive regard. This attitude will bring hope to your group and strengthen your efforts to see and cultivate the best in others.

The Very Beginning

The doors open, the buzz of chatting voices and random laughter fills the room, and suddenly, there they are. Your kids! *Did I do everything I could to make it welcoming? Is it safe, positive, and inviting?* You pause, take a breath, and then remind yourself: *I start the space. It begins with me. It begins with relationships.* You look each of them in the eye, greet them warmly, and begin.

STRATEGIC MOVES

- *Set aside time before your group gathers to breathe deeply. Clear your head of obligations and to-do lists and deliberately move from task mode to relationship mode.*
- *Picture each young person in your group and think of one strength or hope you have for each one. Act from that hope.*

Creating Youth-Friendly Spaces

Youth-friendly spaces have many different aspects—and the spaces themselves are not always physical. We're going to explain how to create a youth-friendly space by focusing on three different aspects that you can think through on the front end so you have a game plan before they even enter into the space. And, then with the decisions made and behind you, you can be fully present for them when the time comes and focus on what truly matters—them. Consider ahead of time how you want to create the following youth-friendly spaces:

A welcoming and inviting space. Eyeball the physical environment to make sure it's hospitable. Also remember to send a message of hospitality in how you engage and interact with youth.

A learning space. Keep in mind how to incorporate assets, brain development, and MIs into your teaching to best engage with your young people.

A leadership space. Think through roles that you can set aside for youth to take on.

A Welcoming and Inviting Space

Be *welcoming.* Create a space that is welcoming and inviting. Let young people help you decorate with posters, lighting, furniture, and paint. Try not to feel hampered by your budget—ask youth and adults to be creative with what you have on hand. Creating a physical space that is youth friendly will help set a vibe for your programming and interactions. And remember the music—nothing says "welcome" like music. Finally, have the space set up as much as possible before programming time, so that when youth come in, the space breathes "You belong here. This is your space. Come and stay a while." This space may be created during the off-programming season (the work before the work!) or at the beginning of a program.

Worried that you can't create this kind of space? No frills? No space of your own? Renting? Borrowing? Taking up a corner of someone else's space? Not to worry. Remember that space isn't just physical; it is also based on a feeling—how youth "feel" about a space is important. Thus, the biggest element in creating a youth-friendly space is to understand that the space you offer really comes from *you*. What counts is how present you are, how much you pay attention, and how understanding you are of your young people's lives. For example, our friends at Community Impact had space in the basement of a building that frequently flooded. They didn't have nice couches, Wii gaming consoles, or fancy paintings on the wall. But the young people embraced the space as *theirs*. Their willingness to own the space had less to do with what was on the walls and more to do with how the youth leader showed up, extended hospitality, and invited the youth to be at home. It had everything to do with making the space inviting, intentional, and relational.

Never underestimate the power of hospitality and invitation. The type of space that tells young people they are welcome and encouraged to truly own and create what is experienced there (be that decorating or rearranging the setting or simply having the freedom to come in, be themselves, and create the energy of the space together).

A friendly, welcoming space also invites youth to come in, make themselves at home, and get active as they enter the room. Set up activity stations that youth can take advantage of as they arrive, before the program gets under way. This lets youth quickly plug into a group and do something of their choice. Establish stations that take into account various multiple intelligences, allow for teamwork and conversations, and suit the interests of your group. For elementary and middle school groups, you might consider stations such as playing Connect Four, building with Tinkertoys, playing Twister, sculpting with play dough, making paper airplanes from recycled paper, or coloring with markers. For high school students, you might have chess, Ping-Pong, darts, Apples to Apples, cards, or Risk. In an academic classroom, you might prepare word problems, trivia questions, or math challenges for small groups to solve.

Interacting in spontaneous small groups helps youth feel comfortable with the people and the activity, and it gives them a chance to do things they enjoy.

EXPANDING YOUTH POWER Let youth brainstorm, design, budget, and create the space. Have your youth choose the activities for each station. Determine station leaders to help get games going and ensure things get under way.

A Learning Space

A learning space is one that values brain development and MIs. A learning space is less physical and more about how you present content and vary what you do. Make sure that you balance your program time through a variety of activities. Vary which young people work together, how, and when. Vary how they work in small groups and large groups. Keep in mind how you balance structured and unstructured play. Include conversations, games, movement, quiet reflection, and online and off-line activities. Variance keeps youth engaged, and it challenges growth in different parts of the brain. Learning space can also mean sharing key information about your agency with youth, so they understand your organization's restraints and mission.

STRATEGIC MOVES

- *Ask youth to teach you about things they know. Show a commitment to shared learning.*
- *Be transparent. When youth come to your program, let them know if you don't have a budget to do certain activities. Learning about your agency and what is on and off limits will help them understand a bigger picture.*
- *Be open to adjusting elements of your program to show young people that they are truly part of the effort, not just passive participants.*

Creating a Space for Sharing Power

In Community Impact's basement space, the leader created a deliberate physical setting to reflect the underlying philosophy of sharing power. The intent of the program and the space was to utilize youth as resources (assets). The leader of the group has the ability to look each young person in the eye to see what's going on and be present to the whole group with no physical barriers separating them. That physical space is intentionally set up as chairs positioned in a circle or a square to communicate that the group is a collaboration of equals.

EXPANDING YOUTH POWER As you seek to create spaces for learning and growing, invite youth to give their input and leadership. Invite them to suggest things they want to learn more about. Invite them to teach or share things they're interested in.

A Leadership Space

You create a leadership space by sharing leadership with youth. Youth can lead in small and large ways. Seeking youth input creates an opportunity for youth and adult partnerships to develop and gives young people ways to practice teamwork and leadership. Do you have opportunities for youth to lead in your program?

Following are suggestions for ways to share leadership with the young people in your program or class. Put a square around all the ideas you believe you could implement.

- Be responsible for maintaining the physical space
- Lead activities and conversations
- Lead check-ins
- Conclude meetings

- Send out meeting communications
- Set the meeting time or set the agenda
- Speak to the group on a given topic
- Plan and lead service opportunities
- Teach the group

STRATEGIC

MOVES

- *If you know youth who are returning to the program, engage them early on and ask them to be prepared to welcome newcomers, lead activities, facilitate small groups, prepare games, or introduce a topic.*
- *If and when they mess up, be ready to support them, help them learn from their mistakes, and let them try again.*

Involving youth as leaders in icebreakers, getting meetings started, or as assistants during activities is a great way to begin expanding power and requires just a little bit of training. Think about how you set up activities with your group. To minimize frustrations, questions, and the potential that your youth will tune you out, set up activities properly and clearly. Teach youth what you know so that they have the confidence to guide and lead.

Consider these guidelines:

- When you go over the instructions, make sure everyone can see you and you can make eye contact with everyone.
- Give clear, understandable directions that are simple and to the point.
- Demonstrate or give an example of what you want done.
- Ask for questions, especially if what you're going to do is tricky or complicated: "Does anyone have any questions about what we're going to do?" or "What are your questions?"
- You may even want to follow up with asking them to tell you what you're going to do next.
- After they start to dig into the work at hand, casually touch base with each person or small group, making sure that they understand clearly and that they are on task and set to succeed.

EXPANDING YOUTH POWER Train youth and let them practice. Let them go! Let youth give the instructions and lead the activities. You can walk around to support, listen in, correct, answer questions, or cheerlead.

Keepers. . . . .

What do you want to remember from this chapter? What might you use or try? Flip back through the chapter and skim for possibilities or keepers. Record the ideas that intrigue you, seem possible, or make you excited.

Connect with Them

Chapter 6

Often in our busyness to "do" our lesson plan or group activity, we can miss the most essential part of our work: our youth. Here we want to look at four keys for connecting with youth and helping them feel they belong. In the upcoming pages, we will explore the power of connection that results from the following practices:

- Welcome and greet your young people
- Know their names
- Invite them to a safe space
- Invite them to a *relational* space

Welcome and Greet Your Young People

What is the first opportunity you have every day to connect with youth? It's to greet them! Walking into a group, especially for the first time, and trying to find a place where you feel welcome can be intimidating. Counter the intimidation by valuing their presence. The moment they enter the door, you have an opportunity to make an authentic connection. As your group enters the room, welcome them and truly be present. This is the time to meet, greet, and assess. Meet them at the door. Greet each one. You can tell a lot about how their day is going simply by looking them in their eyes and greeting them each and every time they show up to your program. As you invite them in, you'll know whether you need to check in further with someone; you'll read the emotions on their faces and know if something is up. This check-in is vital to know whether your group is able to be present or whether something has to be dealt with first before moving on.

Valorie Buck, a youth worker, has some great insights about the importance of helping young people feel welcomed in a program or classroom:

> Welcoming begins with a personal compliment and/or question of interest. I remember being new to a class and never speaking unless spoken to—not because I didn't like anyone. I was simply not in my comfort zone. I can pinpoint exactly the "leaders" who weekly approached me asking me about my home life and complimenting me in one way or another. As a leader at present, I recall those days and remember it's my turn to be proactive—coming out of my shell to speak first—to make others feel comfortable.

Be *specific* in your statements, your compliments, your intentions: How was your swim meet? Did you fix your own hair today—your braids look beautiful! You do not have to intimately know a young person well to be specific in your conversation. But, once you ask questions and get to know a person, you can build on the person's more evident strengths by being even more specific in future conversations.

EXPANDING YOUTH POWER Establish a welcoming crew by putting some of your extroverted youth in charge of welcoming new people or those who recently joined your program. Train your crew to give a tour of your space, to learn newcomers' names, and to initiate some kind of activity with the newcomer. Other welcoming crew members could make a point to say hello to each person in the group, to find something they have in common with people in the group, or to make sure no one is unintentionally left out of a group.

Know Their Names

To build relationships, you have to learn the names of the youth in your program. It seems simple enough but don't underestimate the power of being known by name. Think "Norm" from the television series *Cheers.*

Knowing a person's name is a way of showing honor and respect. When someone tells you her name, repeat it and ask if you are saying it correctly. If you don't get it right the first time, practice until you can say it correctly. Then focus on remembering that name, so you can call the person by name in the future. Taking time to know names communicates value and appreciation. Here are some simple strategies for remembering names:

Repeat names as soon as people introduce themselves. If one person says, "My name is Jim," then respond with, "It's so nice to meet you, Jim." Make a point to use his name again in the conversation. Repetition will cement the name in your memory quickly. (Remember what brain science tells us—you have to repeat to remember!)

Keep a list of young people you interact with on a regular basis. We like to keep this list in a calendar or journal. Sometimes we include the phonetic pronunciation of their names (Shanella = shane + ella) or a phrase to remind us who they are (tall red-headed boy who looks like cousin Jake).

Take pictures of young people in your program, and let them autograph their pictures. Seeing images with the names will help you remember.

Link their names with someone else you know or an object that will help you remember the association. Perhaps Angelica reminds you of an angel. Or George makes you remember your grandpa George.

Combine their names with random facts. You could also ask anything like the following: What color can't you live without? What decade would you want to live in? What kind of car do you want to drive? The more off the wall and less frequently asked the question, the better. The approach keeps youth on their toes, makes them pause, adds in an element of novelty, and helps everyone in the group remember names. Jake Lawrence asks his youth to share their names and what shampoo they use. Random facts create a lighthearted tone and set people at ease. Believe it or not, these crazy facts will also help you remember their names.

Mix movement with the sharing of names. Here's another brain booster from Jake to help your entire group retain names. The first person says, "I'm Weston, and I like to move." Weston then does some sort of move or dance. Everyone else says, "Hey, Weston!" and they copy his move. Continue on to the next person.

Invite Them to a Safe Space

For you to be able to connect with youth and forge relationships of trust, they need to know they are safe: safe in the group, safe to be themselves, safe to share. Creating a safe space goes beyond the prep work we discussed in chapter 5. The dynamics of creating a safe space are active and ongoing and a vital part of connecting with youth. And as we all know, you can't force them to share or "be" themselves. They may choose to wear masks. They may choose to withdraw. Or, they may choose to think they need to put on the "you're an adult, so you're not cool" attitude. Regardless of where they are, we must constantly invite them to a safe space. As we act in our classrooms and programs, we constantly model by our routines—our schedules and norms—that we want them to feel safe.

Routines and Schedules

One aspect of a safe space is the schedule you set up. For your own sanity—and for that of your youth—you also need a routine. There is safety in routines and schedules—they are dependable. Most people like to know what to expect, and they like a general sense of structure, which can help them feel safe and comfortable.

We know you have a general idea of what will happen each day when it comes to your curriculum. Skill-building time on Monday, for example, might be learning to play chess. Tuesday might be a special speaker about the importance of volunteering. Share the general schedule with your group (such as 10 minutes team building, 30 minutes academics, 25 minutes station choices of electives, 10 minutes reflection and sharing). It will give them something to depend on and help ease fears or reluctance. They will know what to expect and be more comfortable. They can manage their energy and the quiet internal stress of the unexpected.

Within your routine, your game plan needs time for flexibility and spontaneity. Flexibility will help you meet youth where they are, pay attention to their needs, and adapt the program to group size. Spontaneity will help you to go with the moment as things arise; for example, you may need to acknowledge those aha moments, prolong the discussion over important questions, or provide a breather if something isn't working. The trick is to be able to balance your general structure with daily variety. Vary the types of activities you lead to engage multiple intelligences and to keep things novel for the brain so that youth stay focused.

Be Intentional with Your Time

As a youth leader, you build your routines around what you need to accomplish, while keeping in mind that your time together is about so much more than just science, band, basketball, or whatever your program is about. If you're running a sports practice, for instance, you might start with basic ball handling skills (dribbling, passing, catching), move into specific drills to practice key skills (with time to introduce concepts and practice), transition into a scrimmage, then finish with a team chant or cheer. All the while, you are using your time together to help your youth grow more than just skills. You are helping them to develop character, learn resistance and social skills, and be respectful.

The Safety of Norms

A safe space to share requires that norms be set up. When you play Monopoly, there are rules. The rules set the boundaries, the goal, the rewards, and the parameters for fun and success. Without the rules, there would be chaos, no sense of direction, and no fun. Being in a group is no different.

For your group to have fun and be productive, you (or your youth) need to set norms for how the group will interact. Everyone needs to understand the rules of what's in bounds and what's out, the goals of the group, the expectations for behavior, the identifiable rewards, and the consequences when people choose to sidestep the rules. As it works for games, so it works for life.

The key to establishing norms is four-fold:

- State and write down the norms in a simple, specific, concise, and positive manner. For example, "Keep your hands and feet to yourself," or "Respect the personal space and personal property of others" instead of "Don't touch others," or "Keep out of other people's things." Accentuate what you're working toward.
- Refer to the norms and use them consistently.
- Post the norms where all can see them.
- Most importantly, develop the norms *together.*

Ownership of the norms happens when youth create the expectations for the group, which includes each of them. When youth help to create the list, they tend to help monitor and uphold the norms, as well as own their own responsibilities in being part of the team.

Setting Up Accountability and Consequences

During the norms conversation, youth may start to dream and declare things they would like to accomplish in the program. The timing is great, because while you're creating norms, you can begin to establish the social contract of accountability and responsibility. Young people can see that you are willing to share power if they are ready to take on accountability. As they come up with things they want to do, you can say, "I'm game for you to do X, but if you want to pull that off, it means you are responsible to make it happen."

In creating the norms *together,* you can also suggest things that are important to you and the productivity of the group. Maybe you have a no-tech zone: no cell phones, iPods, or other electronic gadgets during designated times (which might be the whole time you're together or only for key times). You may also want a "start on time, end on time" rule to honor the time and commitment of everyone involved.

There are multiple methods to engage youth in crafting and upholding norms. We've included several you can use to link norms with active learning, thus engaging more of your young people's thoughtfulness and experiences.

Games for Crafting and Upholding Norms

In and Out Game: Ask the group the following: How are you expected to behave? What rules and expectations are "in" and what rules are "out"? Break your group into two teams: the "In" group and the "Out" group. Give each team five minutes to list the various behaviors expected for their assigned word (*in* or *out*). For example, the In group might say that an "in" behavior is to respect their elders while the Out group might say an "out" rule is whining for what you want. Invite the groups to share their rules out loud. Record their ideas and then, as a group, review and determine the rules and expectations that should be in place for this program and this group.

Game Time: Invite your group to think about a game they like to play—something from childhood, a board game, or a sports game.

Ask them to find partners by calling out their game and clustering with people who chose the same game (or something similar if there is no direct match). Once groups are formed, invite the groups to write down two rules around playing their game along with the consequences if broken. Give them five minutes. When time is up, have each group share their rules and consequences. Record the ideas on a chalkboard, whiteboard, or chart paper. Then invite them to identify rules that could apply to the group as a whole. Remind them to also include rules the group needs so they can have fun and be safe. For example, a rule in basketball is "no fouling." Someone might choose that and say, "Our group needs to have that same rule—no shoving or deliberate provoking of each other. We should play nice." Write down the rules they create and post them where the group can see them frequently.

If–Then Chart: Angie Janssen, a homeschool educator, uses an "if–then" chart. After listing common misbehaviors, the group determines consequences for each infraction. Doing this at the beginning of group time is helpful. Choose a time when you and the group are calm; don't approach this task when you are angry or the group is upset about something. Encourage young people to think through the consequences rationally and help them build critical thinking skills. As with all norms, post it in a common place and follow through when misbehaviors arise.

NOSTUESO: Youth worker Cindy Fee uses the NOSTUESO norm for group conversations. NOSTUESO is an acronym for "**N**o **o**ne **s**peaks **t**wice **u**ntil **e**veryone **s**peaks **o**nce." It's a great way to remind natural talkers to monitor how often they speak and challenge participants who are more quiet to speak up.

You want to be consistent in enforcing norms and setting high ones. Be consistent from person to person from day to day. Make sure that your young people know that you believe in them and that they can be their best. We've all known coaches who make us cringe when they interact with their players. They yell at the top of their lungs, talk down to the players, and demonstratively throw their arms around in disgust as the children play. The players cower in fear. Yelling should never be necessary unless there is an emergency. Love, attentiveness, structure, and accountability are so much more effective. When your youth watch you, what will they see? How will you support norms, set expectations, and be the example?

If at some point your group breaks the norms, remind them of the high standard established in the norms. For example, you might say, "I was just bragging about you. I tell everyone how awesome this group is and how dedicated you are to serving the community (or whatever your group is about), but right now it seems like you're doing the same old thing as other teens. Your behaviors are making a liar out of me." Ask if the norms should be revisited to rethink what the group is about. Always put it back on them. There is power in the safe space the group creates and maintains.

A Few Words about Consequences

You'll note that we covered several ideas on how to establish norms, the importance of having them, involving youth in the decision making about them, and teaching young people to uphold the norms. We did not say, however, exactly what the consequences should be because they are linked to what your group comes up with.

We do suggest that you consider the following general principles regarding consequences. First, let's agree that there should be consequences when norms are violated. And those consequences should be upheld and consistent. (This is where many fall by the wayside.) Establish high expectations (you can do it!). But in setting high expectations and consequences, make sure the consequences match the violation and aren't a ploy for attempting perfection. For example, banning a person from the program for sneaking a whoopee cushion under someone's seat might be a little extreme.

Try this sequence for dealing with challenged norms:

1. When norms are challenged, walk over to where norms are posted and tap the norm in violation.
2. Ask the group what needs to happen next.
3. Do what is necessary (perhaps the simple tap on the norms will get things quiet or you'll need to follow through on a consequence).
4. Ask if they're ready to move on and continue to live by the guidelines they've created.
5. Move on.

Challenge the group to come up with a lighthearted group response when they notice someone violating the norms. You might agree to hum the *Jaws* theme or the first few notes of Beethoven's *Fifth Symphony*, or to tweet like a bird. Drawing attention to the violation in a lighthearted manner will often be all the redirection a young person needs.

A Word about Emotions

Safe spaces in their very nature have an emotional element. Do whatever it takes to create an environment of trust and support. Set a standard for integrity, openness, transparency, forgiveness, and giving people clean slates for "do-overs." Show it by your attitude (expect the best and extend your unconditional positive regard), your actions, what you project, and the expectations you set within your group. You will impact a sense of emotional safety, both within the group and within individuals, when you set and keep norms, expect the best, listen, maintain reliable, calm routines, and continue to believe in who they are. As they feel safe, they learn, engage, and feel permission to simply be.

STRATEGIC **MOVES**

- *Establish norms and set expectations at the beginning of the program.*
- *Honor youth and their feelings. Listen and repeat back in your own words what they are saying, so they know that you have really heard them. Being truly heard is a great gift and goes a long way toward making someone feel valued.*

EXPANDING YOUTH  **POWER** Teach young people to make caring for each other a priority. In a martial arts program in Boston, the instructor keeps a sharp eye on how his students show up. If someone comes in sad, for example, he will pull aside another student and say, "Why don't you go check on him? See what's up." He's training them to be attentive to others and develop empathy, both of which are important aspects of emotional space.

Norms I Hold

Write down the norms that are important to you and how you'd like to uphold them. Norms and rules we love often stem from our values, so think, too, about the values behind the expectations you'll set. It's important for you to know why you're asking certain things from young people.

Journal Exercise

Invite Them to a *Relational* Space

Every kid deserves to be seen, heard, valued, included and loved
by many adults in her/his neighborhoods, families, schools, programs and communities.

—Peter Benson, youth development expert

Perhaps no one says it better than Barney, the beloved purple dinosaur whose
"I Love You, You Love Me" song is forever stuck in our heads. While we
may love or hate the song, the theme is simple and clear. Love. Togetherness. Us. Friendships are the very essence of what we want to create in our
groups. That sense of togetherness and trust where all are welcomed and
known is called relational space and is our ultimate goal. Like safe spaces,
relational spaces are dynamic in nature.

Relationships start with a welcome and with knowing names in a safe
space. They are further built when youth know that you see and care about
them. They know *that* when they know you are present and that *they* are your
first priority. One simple, yet sometimes overlooked, strategy to help convey
that message is to conduct relationship check-ins.

Relationship Check-Ins

A relationship check-in is a simple way to see what's going on in the heads
and hearts of your youth. It works well in group settings because you can
involve everyone and expand the leadership power by letting youth lead
check-ins once they get the hang of how it works (assuming you use the
same method over and over again). Check-ins can also be done one-on-one
and can create room for deeper conversations. The biggest factor in deciding which way to go is time. Either way, your end goal is to ensure everyone
feels like they had a moment to chat if they wanted to.

Consider making relationship check-ins a regular practice. Have a set
time at the beginning of the program (five minutes or so) to chat about the
day and let the young people share what's on their minds and in their hearts.

Some leaders leave this open ended: What's going on? Where's your attention right now? What's going on in the big world and your little world? Other experts shape it in the form of sharing specifics: What's one highlight from the day? What's one place where you're struggling?

Checking in helps set up your entire time together, builds relationships, lets your youth be heard and valued, builds valuable trust, and shows that you put them before any curriculum. As you focus on them and address any concerns, you are able to clear the space and help them relax; from there you can move on to programmatic matters. Check-ins let you be sensitive, real, and show your group that they are your first priority.

> You have to be aware of where your group is and be ready and
> willing to throw the plans and curriculum out the window when
> there are issues to be dealt with today. Forging ahead with your
> plans without acknowledging their issues simply shows that you
> are unaware, or worse, don't really care. Adapting plans and being
> present builds trust and commitment for tomorrow when it is time
> to get back to work. Being present and being flexible are crucial.
> —Anderson Williams, entrepreneur, artist,
> and educational consultant

Miranda, a teenager from Tennessee, likes the way her youth leaders make time for an individual 15-minute check-in with each young person during the program. While the rest of the group is in group time with other leaders, each young person has a moment for deeper relationship building and a chance to share whatever is on his or her mind.

Valorie Buck elaborates on the importance of these individual check-ins:

> The larger our society gets, the more vague and less personal . . .
> I find it more and more appealing to kids to attain one-on-one
> time with the leaders and/or adults. Only then will you find out
> any issues that they may be struggling with and/or be able to
> successfully grow a healthy relationship with them after spending
> this quality time together. The activity does not necessarily have
> to be specific here, but the efforts must be intentional.

Take time throughout the program to connect with each person, even if they seem distant or uninterested, because you never know the impact those simple expressions might have on their attitudes or actions.

EXPANDING YOUTH POWER   **Let youth lead check-in times. Ask youth leaders to let you know when they sense that the group needs extra downtime or conversational space.**

Making Lasting Connections Yourself

It's important that, as the leader, you are able to forge a connection with your youth, not simply facilitate ones among peers. You want to know more than just names and have more than superficial conversations during check-ins. Make efforts to discover what your youth are interested in and what they value. Learn about their strengths and their families. Taking the time to talk with young people lets them see that you genuinely care. If you can find something that you have in common with a youth (you both like the same band, you enjoy going to the same park, or you both like mint chocolate chip ice cream), then you have a relational glue that will help you build bonds and establish a friendship. We find it helpful to keep a list of names and the connections we make with young people. This cheat sheet can be a way for you to track their sparks and interests (read more in chapter 8), consider people or resources you might want to connect them with, as well as provide natural conversation starters for whenever you bump into each other. For example:

> Chantelle: Loves to play soccer; Braves fan.
> Brayden: Avid reader. Currently reading Harry Potter series. Tell B about goodreads.com.
> Louis: Quiet, but loves to talk about chess strategies. Ask if he would like to start a chess club.

Icebreakers

Icebreakers are easy games and activities that get people talking to each other, and they almost always involve some sort of play. You can use them to start the day, transition back from breaks, or whenever you need a pump of energy. Icebreakers can get the group to laugh, help people get comfortable with each other, and add a spark of fun energy to the group. Building relationships needs to be constantly reinforced to maintain connection: you with them; them with each other. Icebreakers, like check-ins, can become a regular part of your programming efforts to continue to build relationships in simple and playful ways. Following are a couple of our colleagues' favorite icebreakers:

Games as Icebreakers

Two Truths and a Lie: Each person shares two truths and one lie about himself or herself. The group tries to guess which fact is a lie. Have them center the two truths and the lie around what happened (and didn't happen) during the course of a week: "This week I ran two miles, I read two books, and I made two new friends. Which one is not true?" This is a great strategy for learning more about what's going on in their everyday lives. (Shared by youth worker Jason Pennington.)

Who's My Homie?: Demonstrate the different elements of homie handshake routines: front slap, snap, back slap, knuckle bump, hand grasp, and hand slide. (YouTube has some tutorials on homie handshakes.) Then, pass out a card to each player with one homie handshake routine on it:

1. Front slap, back slap, snap, vogue/GQ pose
2. Front slap, hand grasp, hand slide, strength pose (arms are gunned to flex muscles)

3. Front slap, back slap, knuckle bump, rapper pose (you make up
   your own rapper stance)

People mingle around, shaking hands with others according to the
homie routines outlined on their cards. Each person should find his
or her "homie match," or the person or people who have the same
routine on their card and then demonstrate their homie handshakes to
the group. Use this to divide your group into pairs or smaller groups,
based on how many matching cards you create. (Shared by consultant
Stephanie Sullivan and counselor Meredith Freeman Middlebrooks.)

Deepen Relationships

As the group begins to gel, you continue to invite them into the relational
space by encouraging them to deepen relationships. Your goal is to create
a sense of belonging within the group that will lead to greater engagement.
Keep providing opportunities for them to learn new things about each other
and to bond. And again, we recommend play as a key strategy for helping you
achieve your goal. Try these ideas to build the group and deepen connections.

Games to Deepen Relationships

Challenge youth to find five things that they have in
common: Examples are an interest in a particular music
style, an affinity for cats, or a love of roller coasters. By
the time they have talked for five minutes, they've progressed beyond the awkward stage of conversation and they have some good
topics for future conversations. This works really well when you're
intentional about challenging old-timers to reach out to newcomers and start the conversation on their own. It's also another way
to expand their power.

Behind Every Name from *Great Group Games*: Have youth gather in triads and ask them to tell the story behind their first name or nickname. Were they named after a family member, or a TV or sports star? Do their names have a cultural meaning? Do they like it? Not like it? Do they have another name they'd rather be called? Give them six minutes to share stories. When done, ask for any interesting things they learned about each other and their names.

Divide your youth into Hogwarts houses (like in the Harry Potter series): Then, let each group design their house shield, color, slogan, and mascot.

Let each group develop their own social media site via Facebook, Instagram, or a blog: (Be sure to check the minimum age requirements.) They can upload profile pictures and stories.

Design miniature clubhouse headquarters with recycled materials: Features should reflect the group's personalities, hobbies, interests, and sparks.

Do team cheers: Coach Terry Ballweber says, "Before games, after games, and at the end of practice, we always try to remember to do a cheer. The kids love it."

EXPANDING YOUTH POWER Let youth lead games. Let them create a list of questions they want to use to learn more about each other.

Mix It Up

As your youth seek to bond as a group, it is important to remember to mix things up. When groups newly form or re-form, they are quickly drawn to familiar friends. This can result in cliques. Try to break those up. When young people exclusively cluster together with certain others, the health of your group is at stake because it leads to some youth feeling uncomfortable and less welcome.

You can strategically facilitate the group identity by continuing to rotate who works with whom so that youth are getting to know multiple people and making new friends.

Monitor the group to see how you need to shake things up. Lead activities in dyads, triads, small groups, and large groups. Using all the different pairings is helpful on different levels beyond creating group identity and breaking up cliques. It mixes up introverts and extroverts, and provides settings in which each can shine. Extroverts love large groups, while introverts blossom in dyads or triads. Mixing it up provides different venues in which learning and growing can take place.

For more persnickety cliques, your strategies might include a simple conversation with the pulse leaders of the cliques, asking them to help create new groups or change up seating arrangements.

Finally, a different way of looking at how to mix it up (and break up cliques) is to focus on MI styles. As you mix up the activities for learning based on styles, you can group participants by their particular MI style. Then, as youth report things outs, have them draw responses, perform skits, or create a written work.

An Unusual Icebreaker

What Color Is Your Tongue?: The most original and unusual icebreaker technique we've heard for mixing up groups is to give a piece of hard candy to each person (use a variety of candy colors) and ask them to put it in their mouths and suck on it. After a few minutes, ask them to stick out their tongues and group by similar colors.

Stay Connected

Youth feel comfortable when they have regular contact with the group. If you have breaks between your meeting times, find a way to keep the group connected. With expanding technology, you have many options, including Facebook, Instagram, e-mail, texting, and an old-fashioned calling tree. Think about events your group can attend. Is someone performing in a play? Playing in the band or a sport? Perhaps your group can go to show support. Balance the importance of being connected with being smart. (Just a reminder that you, as the adult, need to follow your agency's policies regarding contact with youth to keep you and them safe.) Vary the method and stay attuned to each young person's personality and preference to stay in touch, but find a way to stay connected and increase the connection among group members as well.

The Power of Connecting

The impact of simple acts such as greeting, knowing names, and inviting youth into a safe and relational space are often underestimated. We want to close this chapter with a true story that reminds us why these acts are so important.

> Lilly, at 16, has been in and out of group homes and detention centers since coming to America. She has suffered abuse and been a part of many violent situations, both as victim and as instigator. She dealt with the trauma by deadening her emotions. As she shared her history and talked about the trauma and hardship in her life, she showed absolutely no facial reaction. But when she mentioned Big Jim, her demeanor instantly changed. A big smile crossed her face and her eyes lit up as she said, "Big Jim really cared about me." Big Jim owned the detention center where she last spent time.
>
> The interviewer asked, "Do you spend a lot of time with him?"
>
> Lilly responded, "No, but when I came, he opened the door, shook my hand, called me by name, and said he was glad to have me here. I could tell he really cared about me."

That was it. Being greeted, called by name, and welcomed is "the" moment of care that she has and holds on to. The actions in this chapter make a difference, and we don't always know just how much.

 Keepers . . . .

What do you want to remember from this chapter? What might you use or try? Flip back through the chapter and skim for possibilities or keepers. Record the ideas that intrigue you, seem possible, or make you excited.

. . . .

📒 FOR YOUR BOOKSHELF

Find hundreds of icebreakers, mixers, and games in our books: *Great Group Games*, *Great Group Games for Kids*, and *Building Character from the Start*, all of which are available from Search Institute or your favorite bookseller.

Silver Bullets: A Revised Guide to Initiative Problems, Adventure Games, and Trust Activities, by Karl Rohnke (Kendall Hunt Publishing, 2013).

Know Them

Connecting with youth is phenomenal progress, but it's the tip of the iceberg when it comes to positive youth development. In this chapter, we're going to go beyond connecting with youth and cover what it means to really *know* youth. What it means to be in a relationship with your youth. The time you spend getting to know your youth as individuals—their personalities, quirks, cultures, strengths, and needs—is the most important time you will ever spend in your program.

Think about it: What will your youth remember most about you? Will it be the clothes you wore or how you combed your hair? In all likelihood, youth will remember *the kind of relationship you had with them.* More than math equations learned, knots tied, and zip lines crossed, they will remember *whether you cared about them.* The best way to show you care about people is to get to know them.

Relationships are the cornerstone of your program or classroom. Relationships are built on a culmination of experiences, words, actions, body language, and time. Adults often underestimate the power and influence they have on youth. Before we get into strategies, take a moment to think about the people who influenced you. Recall their voice, words, looks of approval or disapproval, hugs, and the nods or shakes of their heads. Recall how much it meant to you to have their approval, support, and care. Who were they? What did they look like? What did they do that made you smile? What mannerisms did you mimic? What drove you crazy?

Who Knew You?

Who was a model for living positive values and a life of integrity?

Who helped you feel good about yourself and your future?

Who helped you feel as if you had something important to contribute?

Who showed you love and simply enjoyed being with you?

What do you remember most about the person(s) who came to mind?

Journal Exercise

EXERCISE

Reflection Time . . . .

Circle the number that best reflects your response to the following statements, with 1 being not so good and 5 being incredibly good.

I look for the good. I look to catch youth
    doing right.   1 2 3 4 5

I help youth find their gifts and strengths.   1 2 3 4 5

I use shared interests/activities to break down
    barriers and help make connections.   1 2 3 4 5

I expect, look for, and cultivate goodness
    or even the idea of it in young people.   1 2 3 4 5

I know when to direct, when to step back,
    and when to let youth lead.   1 2 3 4 5

One of your biggest goals as a youth leader is to develop relationships. The easiest way to do that is to meet young people where they are and as they are. Accept them. Focus on each person with "unconditional positive regard," knowing that each person has the capacity within himself to get to where he needs to be and giving each the space, time, and grace to get there. To help you in this important act, we explore three dimensions for knowing youth well: their personalities, their individuality, and their culture and background. Within these dynamics, you will find tools and ideas to help you really *know* your youth. We hope you will pay special attention to the importance of listening well and playing with your group. Both of these tools go a long way in creating healthy relationships.

Know Their Personalities

We are all wired with unique and distinct personalities that are shaped by who we are, choices we make, and how we respond to the world around us. As you get to know young people's personalities, you will have a better understanding of how they respond to the world and how they communicate.

You will have personalities of every size and shape in your group. Some youth will feel most comfortable when they are on stage in the spotlight. Some will feel most comfortable backstage helping with a project. Some will feel most comfortable with the big group, and some would much prefer one-on-one interactions. Pay attention to the members of your group and respond as much as you can to the way they are wired and how they best receive love. And vary the activities in order to help all feel at ease.

Extroverts versus Introverts—
It's All in the Energy

One aspect of personality is the gathering and presentation of a person's energy, defined as extroverted and introverted. It's important to know who is in your group, so you can balance the social and energy dynamics.

Extroverts are often high-energy, super-social people who thrive on group energy. Extroverts are more comfortable processing their thoughts out loud. In fact, that is their preferred way to process information, and being in a group gives them a rush of energy. Because of how they work best, extroverts tend to get more airtime, and if you are not careful, they can control the whole conversation.

Introverts, on the other hand, are the quieter participants in the group who require more time alone to recharge their batteries. They process internally and thrive on quiet space and time to ponder. Before deciding whether to speak, they will run a conversation or lecture through their heads, filtering facts through an internal conversation, from which they will make a few decisions. If you are not attentive to how they work, you may never hear the brilliant insights or opinions your introverts hold.

EXERCISE

Picture Yourself . . . .

Picture yourself in a group with your own peers. Circle the response below that fits your reaction:

- Being in the group gives me energy. It fills up my energy tank.
- I expend a lot of energy to truly be present in the group. It zaps my energy to be in a group for a long period of time.

Picture yourself at the end of a long day. Which of these options would you reach toward to recharge? Circle the response that fits your reaction:

- Spending time with friends (laughing, chatting, or just being together)
- Quiet time alone (reading a book, being quiet, or taking a walk or a bubble bath)

What are you? If you said that a group gives you energy and you recharge by chatting and laughing, you are probably an extrovert. If you said groups zap your energy and you recharge with solitude and quiet, you are an introvert. Being an extrovert or an introvert is all about how you process information and receive energy most of the time.

Think about your group of young people. How can you support both extroverts and introverts within your group? Think about when you are in a routine discussion and you ask everyone to weigh in. How do you make space for both types to feel comfortable and get their input?

STRATEGIC

MOVES

- *Balance time between energizing group activities and one-on-one pairings or individual work, giving both types time to reenergize.*
- *Nonchalantly pull aside quiet youth and ask them what would make it easier for them to speak up.*
- *Nonchalantly pull aside the talkers and let them know you value their input and ask how they can help bring out ideas from others.*
- *Ask an important question and then tell your group you want them to take some quiet time before weighing in.*
- *Use the NOSTUESO rule to balance power between the types: no one speaks twice until everyone speaks once.*

EXERCISE

Reflection Time . . . .

Circle the number that best reflects your response to the following statements, with 1 being not so good and 5 being incredibly good.

I alter my communication style to fit a young person's personality so that they can truly "hear" me.	1 2 3 4 5
I create a calm environment that youth can rely on.	1 2 3 4 5
I maintain a gossip-free zone with a no-tolerance policy.	1 2 3 4 5
I stick with the facts in difficult conversations and do not shame.	1 2 3 4 5

Be patient. You can't rush people to where you want them to go or grow. You can't make them go there; it is always their choice. All you can do is let them know that there is always that place for them; it's a good place to go and it is safe.

Personality Tests

Helping youth recognize and appreciate their personality quirks and traits can deepen their self-understanding and awareness. There are many personality tools out there, but our favorite is the Smalley Animal Personality test created by Gary Smalley. The animal categories (lions, otters, beavers, and golden retrievers) make the insights easy to remember and are helpful in teaching youth tolerance and acceptance. Knowing each other's temperament can help soften conflict and aid in communication as well as identify natural tendencies for leadership styles. The Smalley Animal Personality test is a great resource for helping your youth better understand themselves and their group while simultaneously building skills.

You can find the free quiz at smalley.cc/free-personality-test/. Note that while this version is for couples, it is easy to use in working with youth. It simply takes some tweaking of the language as you debrief. If you need help in making the transition to using it with youth, e-mail us at cad@theassetedgc.net and we'll be happy to share how we've used this personality test with our groups. After taking the quiz and tallying scores within your group, we recommend this group process to debrief:

1. Divide your group by personality types.
2. Let each animal personality group study the descriptions of their type to learn more about their style, and then ask them to briefly present their type to the rest of the group.
3. Talk about strengths and challenges of each animal personality.
4. Talk about how your group can grow by considering the animal personality styles.

Know Them as Individuals

Every young person is unique and distinctive. There may be overall common personality traits in your group, and knowing personality traits is helpful in giving us insights to how we interact. However, never fall into the trap of boxing young people into a personality type without recognizing the numerous ways in which they are individual and diverse. This bears repeating: *never box them in.* Each young person is uniquely gifted with special sparks, interests, purpose, and way of showing up. Get to know and enjoy that one-of-a-kind package that makes up each of the youth in your group.

STRATEGIC

MOVES

- *Create a list of questions your group can use for simply having conversations together.*
- *Consider having one-on-one conversations with each youth to find out some personal goals each wants to set.*
- *Find out what interests your youth and how they enjoy spending their time. Whenever possible, let their talents shine in the group.*

Uniquely Me

Uniquely Me from *Great Group Games for Kids*:
This game highlights what's unique about each person.
On each index card numbered 1–4, each person writes
down 1) something about her appearance today (wearing red, have
on a hoodie), 2) something about her character (I love to laugh;
I value honesty), 3) something unique about her (I can blow a
bubble in a bubble; I play the harmonica), and finally 4) her name.
Everyone is asked to stand. The leader starts reading the cards,
one by one. People sit down when the descriptors don't apply to
them anymore.

Listen Well

Listening is really *the* key to both connecting with and knowing youth on
an individual level. Nothing beats truly listening. Hands down it is the
number one thing you can do to help youth know you care about them.
Listening is a huge part of supporting young people and building relationships. Don't let yourself slip into the habit of listening halfway, while you
are really thinking about something else. Resist the urge to interrupt with
what you think they should do or by sharing your own story. Give young
people your full attention—look them in the eyes, ask thoughtful questions
about what they are sharing, and learn to "listen between the lines."

Effective listening carries through in how you respond. Avoid using *but*
in your responses *(I agree but . . .)* because the word creates an emotional bar-
rier in conversations. Instead, ask them to tell you more about it. Oftentimes,
more is communicated through facial expressions, body language, and tone
of voice than the words alone. Being a good listener means being fully present and fully attentive. And, it's an opportunity to model good listening
skills for youth, as they learn to effectively communicate with others.

As you listen to young people share, you will begin to see through their words and into their hearts. Thoughtfully respond to the words they are saying and the feelings they are expressing by using some of these phrases that young people long to hear. *"I am here for you. I believe in you. I care. I understand. I'm listening. Let's do it together. Everyone makes mistakes. You can have a new start. What do you think? How can I support you? You are good enough. Believe in yourself. I'm grateful for you. You can do it."* But only speak words that are true for you, because the youth will see right through insincerity and begin to question your motives.

EXERCISE

✎ Reflection Time . . . .

Circle the number that best reflects your response to the following statements, with 1 being not so good and 5 being incredibly good.

I listen so young people truly feel heard.   1 2 3 4 5

I take time to *simply chat and be.*   1 2 3 4 5

I express interest in life outside of the program.   1 2 3 4 5

I know when to toss the plan to *focus on what's real*
   with youth.   1 2 3 4 5

I find out the little things about them and weave them
   into conversations or activities: favorite candy bars,
   birthdays, favorite music, favorite movies.   1 2 3 4 5

Remember the importance of creating relational space. Let your kids know that you care. Everything stems from that fact.

Silence Is Our Friend

As you listen to youth, make sure you invite silence into the conversation. Some of us hurry conversations because silence makes us uncomfortable. Silence, however, is a friend to conversations and creates space for introverts to think and for everyone to reflect. After you ask a question, wait 10–12 seconds (count: one Mississippi, two Mississippi, three Mississippi, and so forth) before you ask another question. Or breathe slowly in between. These two tricks will help you slow down and focus on them.

Initial Thoughts

When have you been guilty of half-listening lately?

To whom do you need to listen more intentionally?

Are there words of encouragement that you need to share with someone who has recently shared their thoughts and feelings with you?

How can you be a better listener?

Journal Exercise

Know Their Culture and Background

Part of knowing your youth is knowing where they come from—their cultural backgrounds as well as the distinct nature of youth culture and norms. Youth identify themselves in many ways. They may define themselves by dress, interests, music, economic class, ethnicity, physical challenges, learning differences or learning styles, sexual identity, being technologically bilingual, and so many more aspects that make each of us unique and different.

Even with these differences, you and your group must recognize that every child is valuable and has innate gifts. When someone is labeled "different"—be that from identity, ethnicity, abilities, or even personality quirks—the space we create within our group needs to be strong and supportive and free of prejudices, offering hospitality, acceptance, and appreciation for each young person.

Initial Thoughts

Do I have any stumbling blocks in working with various youth? Do I have a place of discomfort or prejudice that I need to examine that may get in the way of *me* offering acceptance and love?

Why is it important for me to understand youth culture and the various ways youth self-identify?

Journal Exercise

How Culturally Savvy Are You about Your Group?. . .

Quiz yourself to see how up you are on your young people's heritage and youth culture. Read through each set of subquestions and highlight the three that are most meaningful to you.

How well do you . . . know them?

Do you know what name they want to go by—their given name or a nickname?

Do you know how to pronounce it correctly?

Do you know their skills and interests?

Do you know whether they have food allergies? Are any sick with a critical illness? Are any on medications?

Do you know whether they have experienced a personal trauma?

Do you know whether they have a learning difference?

Do you know their MI bent?

How well do you . . . know their world?

Do you know what their primary, first language is?

Do you know the current trends in youth dress?

Do you know the cultural requirements of their dress (dresses, covering faces . . .)?

Do you know their rituals and traditions?

What's the popular manner for greeting each other? Knuckle bump? Something else?

Do you know their music? What are the top five songs/bands/ groups your group is listening to?

Do you know the social media venues they use to keep up with each other?

Do you keep up with the books, movies, and art interests that appeal to your age group?

How well do you . . . know their family life?

Have you met their parents?

Do you know what the family rules are—the ones that might impact rules you set in your program or classroom?

Have you asked about their family traditions?

Do you know whether the family is going through something serious such as a divorce, loss of a loved one, or other major trauma?

How well do you . . . know their spiritual and cultural practices?

Do you know whether they must pray at a certain time each day?

Do you know whether they must avoid certain foods?

Do you know whether they are allowed to touch (shake hands, do a high five) a member of the opposite sex?

Do you know how they approach holidays? (What holidays do they celebrate? Are any holidays taboo?)

Do they have meaningful holidays that you should know about?

Sometimes religious or cultural practices might impact what you do or how you conduct your program. Once you learn them, you can be flexible and adjust your rules so that your rules don't stifle their cultural identities.

. . . .

Five Keys to Being Culturally Sensitive

Following are some important guidelines to help you be culturally sensitive with your youth.

1: Always remember that kids are kids. No matter what their heritage, background, self-identification, or what is going on in their lives, *kids are kids.* When you remember that, the "difference" that you're dealing with fades to the background and you will focus on what's really important about a young person. Chad Harrington, a youth worker with Nations Ministry Center, reminds us, "The refugee middle schoolers with whom I work are just like other American students. The biggest difference is that their struggles are simply magnified: social ostracism, academics, and hormones—all present challenges—just more so because of all the cultural differences."

2: Protect the uniqueness of each young person. Don't let misconceptions breed rampant and destroy your group. Stay educated, educate others, and maintain the norm of respect. Create opportunities for youth to learn and grow together so they can experience "difference" and see that "different" isn't that different. Consultant Kelli Walker-Jones advocates that we "stay curious enough not to label them. The point is to see them as a kid, love them, and help them grow. If you don't know something about them, whether it is Tourette's syndrome, their cultural traditions, or what it means to be lesbian, gay, or transgender, then find out. Get curious and educate yourself for the sake of understanding them personally and being able to offer them support."

3: Help youth find what they have in common. Discovering commonalities covers a lot of ground in bridging gaps created intergenerationally or even culturally, and it creates a solid base to explore differences and how each person is unique. Anything can be bridged once you establish how youth are alike. And, no surprise, our number one strategy in finding common ground is by using games as the platform to facilitate that discovery.

4: Remember that you are the role model. Set a norm for respecting one another, even if you don't understand or fully agree with some of the

Be Aware of Bullying

Be on the lookout for silent or flagrant bullying based on any differences in the group and teach your youth to do the same. Immediately deal with bullying. No one should ever be ridiculed or teased because of who they are.

views. If you have a moment where you feel uncomfortable about a viewpoint, action, or self-identification, stop and do a self-check. Is your reaction from a prejudice? Is it from a lack of knowledge, experience, or understanding? Get yourself a check-in first and then be the model for creating a supportive, loving environment where everyone is valued and accepted.

5. Be deliberate in finding ways to highlight cultural and self-identification differences as assets to the group. Make sure every unique characteristic has a way to rise up as an asset to the group. Invite youth to share their views, traditions, and culture related to any given topic: cooking, music, art, stories, games, dance, and holiday or religious traditions. Find ways to let your youth lead workshops or teach others about what they know or can do. They can share things such as what it's like to be Muslim, what it's like to grow up in Indonesia, what it's like to have a chronic illness, or what it's like to speak two languages. Everyone has something to bring and offer to the group to make it stronger. When you tap into the strengths of who they are, their experiences, and what they're good at doing, you create the space for them to share power and build understanding.

Including Diverse Perspectives

One of the young people we worked with came from a communal culture. He had an unbelievable perspective and knowledge about how community works that was very different from how the other kids viewed community. His youth leader asked him to write a paper and then lead a workshop for his peers to help them understand the power of community as he saw it.

STRATEGIC

MOVES

- *Check the verbal and nonverbal messages you are sending.*
- *Be mindful that many immigrants have faced significant trauma.*
- *Use transitional downtimes or bus times to share cultures by inviting youth and adults to introduce their favorite music, traditions, foods, or games.*
- *Educate yourself if you're at a loss. Knowledge is power.*
- *Explore and know your cultural heritage and background.*

Who Are You?

PLAYFUL MOVES

This activity, developed by Sharon Williams, a seasoned youth services professional, lets youth explore their identity. Get into pairs. One participant will be the "questioner"; the other will be the "respondent." When the facilitator says "go," the questioner asks, "Who are you?" The respondent answers with a descriptor of themselves ("I am a brother," "I'm a gamer"). The questioner asks the question again, "Who are you?" and the respondent answers with a different descriptor. The questions and responses continue until the facilitator calls time (after about 60–90 seconds). When time is called, the partners switch roles. Afterward, debrief them with the following questions:

1. Did you learn something new about your partner?

2. What things do you have in common?

3. Looking at the different things that make you "you," what are you most proud to be?

Take Time to Listen and Learn

Terri Lawson, Family Resource Center director, shares the story of a group of youth from Somalia who would disappear into the bathrooms each day at school to wash up. They were unsupervised, making a lot of noise, and left the bathrooms a filthy mess, all of which caused staff complaints. One of the staff eventually learned that the Muslim youth had to pray at certain times each day, and their faith required that they wash their face, hands, and feet before prayer. Once they understood this behavior, the staff addressed the issue, so that the center could honor the students' beliefs and the students could respect the center's need for quiet, as well as learn the importance of cleaning up after themselves.

Keepers. . . . .

What do you want to remember from this chapter? What might you use or try? Flip back through the chapter and skim for possibilities or keepers. Record the ideas that intrigue you, seem possible, or make you excited.

FOR YOUR BOOKSHELF

"Extroversion or Introversion," The Myers & Briggs Foundation, www.myersbriggs.org/my-mbti-personality-type/mbti-basics/ extraversion-or-introversion.asp.

"Quiet Quiz: Are You an Introvert or an Extrovert?" Susan Cain: The Power of Introverts, www.thepowerofintroverts.com/quiet-quiz-are-you-an-introvert/.

The Treasure Tree: Helping Kids Understand Their Personality, by John and Cindy Trent and Gary and Norma Smalley (Thomas Nelson, 1998).

"Personality Types: Lion, Otter, Golden Retriever, and Beaver." WeirdGuy, weirdblog.wordpress.com/2007/02/22/personality-types-lion-beaver -otter-and-golden-retriever/.

"The TypeFinder Personality Test," Truity, www.truity.com/test/ type-finder-personality-test.

Conversations on the Go: Clever Questions to Keep Teens and Grown-Ups Talking, by Mary Alice Ackerman (Search Institute Press, 2004).

Ask Me Where I'm Going & Other Revealing Messages from Today's Teens, By Ruth Taswell (Search Institute Press, 2004).

Tag, You're It!: 50 Easy Ways to Connect with Young People, by Kathleen Kimball-Baker and Kathryn (Kay) L. Hong (Search Institute Press, 2003).

The 5 Love Languages of Children, by Gary Chapman and Ross Campbell (Moody Publishers, 2012).

"Discover Your Love Language," The 5 Love Languages, www.5lovelanguages.com.

Bullying at School: What We Know and What We Can Do, by Dan Olweus (Wiley-Blackwell, 1993).

Make a World of Difference: 50 Asset-Building Activities to Help Teens Explore Diversity, by Dawn C. Oparah (Search Institute Press, 2006).

Words Wound: Delete Cyberbullying and Make Kindness Go Viral, by Justin W. Patchin (Free Spirit Publishing, 2013).

"Ages and Stages," ParentFurther, www.parentfurther.com/ages-stages.

Engage Them

Each of us has a fire in our heart for something. It's our goal in life to find it and to keep it lit.

—Mary Lou Retton, Olympic gymnast

Research tells us that as human beings, we are hardwired to connect with others and find meaning and purpose. We are wired to have and create purpose for ourselves. The secret is to find out what is meaningful for each of us, so we can be "possibilitarians." We all desire to cast a vision of what can be and who we will be when we are doing what means the most to us.

You've seen how young people yearn for life to have significance. They want their life to matter. They have energy and a sense of possibility; the negative side of "experience" hasn't trapped them by failures that sometimes breed cynicism. They still believe anything is possible.

One of the greatest gifts we can give young people is to help them discover and feed into that inner fire within, the one that gives them meaning, purpose, and a greater sense of self and their place in this world. Purpose is that "something" that gets you up in the mornings and makes you excited about life. It gets you moving. It gets you engaged.

Once young people have started to explore and discover their own skills, talents, personalities, and passions, they need to find ways to put those strengths to work—to make beautiful things, to invent, to create, or to make a difference in their homes, neighborhoods, schools, and communities by giving of their best selves, talents, and energies. Like building muscles in the body, youth's strengths will grow stronger as they use them, and their communities will grow stronger as well.

In this chapter, we provide some kick-starters and strategies for helping youth find and engage with their sense of purpose. We'll look at the conditions we can create and what we can do based on three recommended strategies: talk, explore, and connect.

Before we begin to work through these strategies, we want to offer a word of friendly caution. This chapter is very much a "practice" chapter and full of tools. It will be tempting to grab an activity and put it to immediate use. Resist that urge. This chapter is all about young people figuring out and engaging with the heart of their power—their purpose. You want them to start to look for it and be aware that it's important information for them to know. So, don't get so excited about leading the activities that you forget the overall goal of building young people's capacities and strengths and expanding power. As you read through various options and strategies, ask yourself the following questions:

1. Which activities do they already know how to lead?
2. Which activities can they lead if I give them a copy of directions to read beforehand?
3. Which activities do I need to train youth in small groups before they can lead with the others?

Enjoy the journey as you begin to help them discover their passions and purpose.

TAKE 2 TWO The journey of self-discovery starts with you! To help young people discover their inner fire (which leads to living a life full of purpose), we have to first know what gets us out of bed in the mornings. If we can't share what we love and what gives our lives meaning, how can we expect them to begin to see something larger, grander than themselves?

Purpose is rooted in passion. Your passion is the bug that infected you. What is your passion? When is it that you feel most alive and so big inside that the world isn't big enough to hold you? What do you love doing? Who helped you figure out that *this* is your thing, the thing that gives you joy and life?

. . . .

Talk

By talk, we mean an honest-to-goodness two-way conversation you can have with youth that inspires them to think about what matters most to them. Talk involves asking questions, lots of questions. Don't assume answers based on what you think you know about your youth. Ask questions and let them tell you. Take time to listen to their responses. You just may be surprised at what they have to say.

Use the questions from the Take Two exercise to start the same conversation with your youth. Ask them questions to get them thinking about passions and interests. You might very well be the person who helps them "catch the bug" for (fill in the blank: writing, art, singing, martial arts, making furniture) because you share your enthusiasm and passion for what you love to do. Or, you may be the person who opens the door and helps them find out what truly makes them excited.

So, begin the conversation. It doesn't have to be hard. You can start simply by comparing different interests, how much each one matters to each of you, and why. Or the conversation can be embedded within an activity to make it fun and engaging. You'll notice in the activities we've shared that we vary the methods and techniques, but we keep to the theme of talking about sparks and asking the pertinent questions. We do it in multiple ways and from different angles, knowing that if you do these activities, the message—or the question—will start to percolate and the answers will bubble forth. And that's the goal.

What's Important to Me. . . . .

Ask youth to use one of three hand motions to indicate their choice as you call out activities. If the activity called out is something that matters a little to them, they should hold their index finger and thumb close together; if it is something that matters somewhat, they should hold both hands a little distance away from each other in front of their chest; if the activity is something that matters a lot to them, they should spread their arms wide apart from their bodies.

- Trying new things
- Going to the movies
- Being a good friend
- Being outside
- Having time to play
- Volunteering
- Hanging out
- Tech time
- Celebrating achievements
- Helping or being with animals

- Spending time alone
- Reading books
- Spending time with family
- Having time to be creative: music, arts, building
- Playing a sport

As you call out the various activities, notice where everyone is on the spectrum. Take time to stop after different activities to ask why a particular activity matters a little, somewhat, or a lot. You can have people turn to a neighbor to share or facilitate answers as a big group.

. . . .

Exploring Personal Passions

Sparks Speedy Conversations modified from *Get Things Going:* Use these questions to jump-start thinking about what gets everyone excited about being alive. We use this activity in speedy conversation rounds where participants form two lines (facing each other) and each pair has time to talk about one question before one line rotates to form new pairs and get new questions. Use as many or as few questions as you like, or use them in different sessions.

What makes you laugh out loud?

When do you feel most alive?

What gives you energy (beyond sleep and caffeine)?

What gets you up out of bed and excited for the day?

What screensaver/wallpaper/Pinterest page would best describe your interests?

What is a dream you have for your life?

What is the impact you want to have on the world?

What is your day like when you get to do the thing you love most?

Debrief:

What did you learn about yourself from this activity?

Did you see any themes in your answers that kept cropping up? Did you find yourself talking about the same thing over and over?

My Sparks . . . .

Note: This activity works best when it follows a warm-up activity such as What Matters to Me, Sparky Choices (on page 127), or Sparks Speedy Conversations. Those activities let your youth think about sparks in general ways before they dive in to name their sparks.

Share the following quote with your youth (note: the source is anonymous): *"Each of us is wired with a different type of magic within us. Discover the magic within yourself."* Then, define "sparks." Explain that a spark is that magic within each of us. Sparks express themselves as talents, passions, gifts, or beliefs. They give us energy, motivation, focus, and happiness. They make us feel alive. Sparks are what give our lives meaning and purpose. They motivate. They help us get out of bed in the mornings.

Invite your youth to write down on an index card their sparks, the passion(s) that makes them come alive with joy when they are engaged in it. (If some young people have trouble writing a spark, ask them a few questions to help them think about it. Find sample questions in the activity "Exploring Personal Passions through Sparks Speedy Conversations.") After a moment of reflection, invite youth to hold their cards outward in front of them so that everyone can see what they wrote. Invite participants to form groups based on similarly shared sparks (for example, writing and drawing might pair up because they share a common creativity element). Help facilitate group pairings as needed.

Once your youth are in groups, look at the variety of sparks within each group. Share that Search Institute has revealed that research on youth has identified more than 200 sparks, limited only by imagination. Jim Conway, a Search Institute workshop leader, emphasizes that what is important is that each person has a spark inside, something that makes him or her beautiful, good, and useful to the world. The discovery of our sparks helps us get on the road to discovering our purpose.

Finally, invite the small groups to share stories of their sparks. Ask them questions: Why is this spark important to you? How did it come to be an important part of who you are? How might you integrate your spark into extracurricular activities, volunteer opportunities, and future careers? How can you use your sparks in life? Give them 10 minutes to share stories.

The Research on Sparks

During the past decade, Search Institute has been studying young people who are thriving—not just surviving, not just getting by, but who are truly doing well and are aware of and using their interests, talents, and abilities; achieving their goals; and living up to and beyond their potential. Search Institute discovered three things that, when present in young people's lives, almost guarantee that they will thrive:

1. Young people know their "sparks," the special interests and abilities they are passionate about.
2. They pursue their sparks and use them to contribute to a better world.
3. Their parents and other adults support, encourage, and help them with their sparks.

And guess what? The research tells us that young people can almost always name their sparks. They get it. They know exactly what we're talking about.

Take two minutes to write down two things you want to make sure you remember about sparks.

. . . .

Questions: The Groundwork for Using Sparks to Discover a Sense of Purpose

Asking questions is the key to digging deeper and getting beyond "sparky moments," which are typically easy for kids to name. But you (and they) need to get to purpose, or the basis for those sparks, and the best way to do this is by asking questions, repeatedly, until you've struck gold:

Why those interests?
Why that activity?
What's the motivation behind a given activity?

If you keep asking "why?" you push the envelope to get at the underlying values beneath their choices. You raise their self-awareness and understanding of what makes them tick. Knowing their motivators (the sparks they identify) makes it easier for them to see how they are wired. When youth do what they love and it aligns with their values, they are on the road toward leading a full and fulfilling life.

Questions to Help You "Talk"

Following are three takes on how to use questions to engage youth in a deep conversation about their sparks and get them to reveal their purpose.

1. Ask questions around activities:

> Is this really fun for you?
>
> Have you always been good at this or did you have to learn it first?
>
> What do you like about it?
>
> Do you have any goals around this? Anything I can do to help?
>
> I love seeing you doing well and enjoying it.

Next, help them see how they can connect their spark to life. For example, if they are good at spelling words, encourage them to enter a spelling bee or help a friend study for a spelling test. Open their eyes to possibilities.

2. Notice when youth are having an experience where they light up and stay that way, when they are so into the thrill of what they are doing that "time doesn't exist." Following are some signs of sparks: Eric just spent two hours in front of the computer editing video footage and then proudly showed others the resulting five-minute clip. Mary, who has been bored through the first month of science class, suddenly lights up when you start talking about the ocean. When you see your youth light up, consider asking some of the following questions to help them explore more:

> What does it feel like when you're doing this activity?
>
> How did you become so motivated?
>
> Do any of your friends like doing this, too?
>
> How can we figure out a way for you to do more of this?
>
> Would you teach me a little about it so I can share in the fun or
> better understand what you're talking about?
>
> What are the things you like about it?
>
> How does a person move to the next level?
>
> Is there anything else that makes you feel this way?

Noticing when youth are happy is a great way to affirm their spark and what is special about them. Check back in as follow-through: Have you found a book to read that is as good as Harry Potter? When is your next poetry reading?

3. Make sure to talk about your sparks and what made *your* day happy. Come in and share the great parts of your day to engage in a conversation. Then ask them questions about theirs. Teach them to look for the good and to value it.

> When is the last time you had a day like that?
> What were you doing? What was so great about it?
> [If it has been a while] What could we do to make tomorrow or the next day a day like that for you? What would you want to do? How would you spend your time?
> I don't always have days like this, but I love it when I do—and it happens more often when I do what I love. What do you love to do?

Explore

We can help youth identify for themselves their best moments and begin to think about who they are and what makes them tick by creating moments and offering activities in our programming time to try new things. As you offer activities, look for the "hot spots," those moments when a majority of your youth get excited and sustain that reaction. If possible, offer more opportunities around those spark flashes to further engage them.

Sparky Choices. . . . .

Find out what makes your group excited to learn and participate. Instruct your group to rate each of the following choices you give them by making these gestures:

- If they think the choice is "hot" and definitely interesting, ask them to fan their faces as if they are overheating.
- If they think the choice is uninteresting and they feel "cold" toward the choice, ask them to rub their arms as if they are freezing and need to get warm.
- If they are unsure about the choice, ask them to throw their palms up and shrug their shoulders.

Read aloud several of the options from the "Sparky Choices" activity page for youth to respond to. Pay attention to their reactions and make notes on strong reactions.

Next, work with your group to add to the list things they would like to experience or do in their lives. Star the ones you can do with your group. Note where you can make connections between their passions and what you're teaching in your classroom or program. How can you help them explore more?

Spark Identifier	Spark Reaction Notes
Ride a roller coaster eight times straight	
Build a doghouse	
Design a building	
Put together an engine	
Make a new smoothie flavor	
Have one of my stories published	
Teach in a school in another country	
Dig in an archaeology site	
Ride an elephant	
Do a political analysis for a major news station	
Find a solution to climate changes	
Do interior design	
Start my own business	
Coach an Olympic team	

When done, challenge youth to create their own personal Spark Vision List of things they would like to experience or do in their lives. What appeals to them? What sounds fun, intriguing, challenging? Why?

Sparks Walk

Add a new twist to the old game Take a Hike: Invite participants to sit in a circle of chairs facing each other. There should be one less chair than the number of people in the group. That extra person stands in the middle and starts the game.

Introduce the concept of passion and sparks by asking them to think about all the things they truly love to do or would love to try. Play begins when the circle leader says, "Take a walk if you love to . . ." and completes it by saying something he or she loves to do. (Examples might be "hike," "travel to Italy," or "play the drum.") Everyone who shares that interest must take a walk and find a new seat in the circle; this includes the leader. Participants are not allowed to simply take one seat to the left or right; they must scramble for their new spot. The person who doesn't find a new space becomes the new circle leader and calls out the next "take a walk" statement (which must be something he or she loves).

Afterward, talk about the variety of dreams that people have and the activities that people love to do. Ask them to identify which of the activities or dreams they named that they are currently pursuing. Use the time to brainstorm and set goals for following their passions. Who do they know who could help them get involved in tuba lessons, flower arranging, or car maintenance, for example? Where are there opportunities to explore these interests in the community? Are there classes?

Using the Arts to Explore Sparks

Visuals can give expression to feelings and interests that words can't express. Music can reveal emotions and aspirations better than simple words. Poetry can capture hearts, imaginations, and minds, giving us new understanding. The arts can expand our view and help us see our experiences and the world through new eyes. Collect photos, songs, and poems to use as prompts to help youth explore purpose and passion.

STRATEGIC **MOVES**

- *Let youth use Pinterest or Instagram to craft a visual story of the things that are important to them.*
- *Use picture books to engage with youth to explore a variety of topics. Peter H. Reynolds's* The Dot *illustrates how a teacher helps a student discover a hidden talent.*
- *Use music from YouTube, Pandora, Songza, or Spotify to engage in conversations about passions and purpose. (And, as you'll recall from chapter 3, music feeds the brain as well!) What message does the music hold? What song would they choose to represent their values? Their purpose? The difference they want to make?*
- *Share poems or quotes written by youth or adults that speak to passion, purpose, and possibilities.*

Create Opportunities to Explore Spirituality

Meaning and purpose can often take the form of spirituality for many people, which in essence has us circling back around to the underlying theme of this chapter: the importance of knowing one's motivation and sense of purpose. Even if you are not working in a faith-based setting, it's important to help youth explore their spirituality, their reason for existence, their sense of personal values, and the pillars that strengthen and support them. It's another dimension of purpose and meaning.

Spirituality is *anything we do to connect with the largeness of life*. In practice this can run the gamut from time in the great outdoors to any number of approaches to prayer and meditation to respectful practices of being together to listen, worship, praise, reflect, and so forth.

—Rick Jackson, educational consultant

Let's Talk about It . . . .

Set aside some time to talk about spiritual experiences and practices. Ask the group to make it safe and comfortable for all to talk by agreeing to take turns, speak only about one's own beliefs, and listen respectfully. Following are some potential discussion questions:

- How do you know if you're a good person?
- Why are you here, alive on the earth right now?
- Do you feel more spiritual when you're alone or when you're with other people?
- How does having lots of material things make it easier or harder to be spiritual?
- What is the source that never fails you and always gives you peace and help?
- What is your favorite motto to live by?
- What is a favorite holiday, festival, or ritual? Why?

Nurturing Your Own Spirituality

People use many different practices to help themselves grow spiritually. Take a look at the chart and rate how important these practices are for you: Circle 1 for very important, 2 for somewhat important, or 3 for not important at all.

Spiritual Practice	How Important Is It to You?		
Listening to music	1	2	3
Prayer	1	2	3
Meditation	1	2	3
Reading the Koran, the Torah, the Bible, or other sacred texts	1	2	3
Having a deep conversation with a friend	1	2	3
Attending a religious service or class	1	2	3
Spending time in nature or with animals	1	2	3
Holding or looking at a sacred object	1	2	3
Singing or chanting	1	2	3
Dancing, practicing yoga or tai chi, or another physical practice	1	2	3
Creating art or playing a musical instrument	1	2	3

Other:

Discuss

- Do you do certain practices only in groups or only when by yourself?
- Do the practices you find important have qualities in common?
- Choose one of the practices you do and share with the group a story of when this practice has been especially meaningful to you.

Connect

Twenty years from now you will be more disappointed by the things that you didn't do than by the ones you did do. So throw off the bowlines. Sail away from the safe harbor. Catch the trade winds in your sails. Explore. Dream. Discover.

—Mark Twain, author

As you see their sparks and interests, connect your youth with other supporters and opportunities to further explore and develop their interests. Never underestimate the power of noticing, naming, and pointing out their passions and complimenting them on what they enjoy doing. Observe. Support it and tap into it. And remember to encourage young people to be brave and try new things. It's easy for people to get stuck in a rut, doing the same things they have always done. Sometimes that stems from complacency, insecurity, or fear. Challenge your youth to be adventurous and bold. If they express fear about something they have always wanted to try, ask them to consider these questions:

- What's the worst thing that could happen if you tried it?
- What's the best thing that could happen if you tried it?
- What would give you the courage to try it?
- How can I or other adults support you in your adventures?

Sometimes that little push is all a young person needs. Remember that for some young people, trying new things is a scary adventure. Be the cheerleader and the encourager as you guide them into the unknown. They just might discover a whole new part of themselves along the way.

The quality of your life is the quality of your relationships.

—Anthony Robbins, motivational speaker

Life is not meant to be lived in silos. As we mentioned at the beginning of this chapter, humans are hardwired to connect with others. Young people benefit from meeting different people and working side by side on projects as they engage in service and conversation. Find a way to generate interactions with people of various cultures, ages, and lifestyles. Bring them into your classroom or program, plan activities to do with them, visit people who are different from your youth in some way. Teach youth to respect others, even if they are incredibly different, even if they disagree with their lifestyles. Respect does not equal agreement; it's an attitude of honoring another person because every person has value.

STRATEGIC MOVES

- *Invite other staff to share their sparks, and make them aware of the interests of your particular youth. This way, other adults can offer encouragement and build connections with your students. Encourage conversations. Encourage questions.*
- *Consider bringing older adults into your building for an intergenerational talent show, a painting class, or a Martin Luther King Day event.*
- *Invite families to bring babies, toddlers, teens, and grandparents to your program often, so you can get to know them. Encourage cross-age mentoring, reading clubs, or nature walks together.*
- *Plan quarterly field trips or do service projects side by side with youth from a refugee center or a school for children with disabilities.*
- *Challenge your youth to continually seek relationships through which they can grow and help others grow. Relationships are transformational—they are the source of constant character development.*
- *Connect youth with classes and people who share similar sparks and interests. If they are interested in cooking, for instance, help them find out about cooking resources around town and online.*

As you seek to connect youth with others, help them realize that they are part of something much bigger than just themselves. Open your group's eyes to the wealth of support, opportunities, needs, and ideas in your organization, your community, your state, and around the world. Invite guest speakers who can share what they do, why they love it, and how they follow their passions to make a difference in the world.

TAKE TWO 1. What opportunities do you provide in your program time for youth to discover and explore their sparks?

2. What about yourself? Do you make time to explore your own sparks?

. . . .

Create Opportunities for Youth to Serve

Serving connects youth not only to people in the community but also to career and vocational ideas. Options for serving the community are endless. Consider on-site projects such as cutting fleece baby blankets for newborns, making trail mix for homeless people, or painting pictures for hospice patients. Consider off-campus projects such as pulling nonnative plants in a local park, serving a meal in a homeless shelter, or leading games in an after-school care center. As youth start to find their sparks for service, they can delve deeper, exploring long-term volunteer opportunities with organizations. See what service options are available in your community to expose youth to serving from their sparks and connecting to others at the same time.

Ellen Zinkiewicz, a workforce development professional, suggests that volunteer experiences can provide young people with insights about future careers and vocations. After the service experience, ask youth, "What jobs did you see the people at the site doing today?" If you talk with adults from the agency, encourage youth to ask about their career stories. What was their journey to the job they are in now? What kind of training or education did they need? How did they learn that the job or that kind of work even existed?

Places That Need My Sparky Self

Fill in the blanks.

Name

My top skills/talents

My sparks

How *could* I use my talents/skills/strengths/sparks to impact the world?

The way I want to serve others and/or the project I want to start:

As you get an idea of the passions and interests your youth have, look at connecting them to places where they can serve by using their sparks to make things better. Explore together possible agencies or places that fit their hearts and interests.

As youth go out and serve, ask them afterward about their experiences and encourage them to keep a simple journal to record what they did, how they felt about it, what they learned, and how they put their talents to work. Ask: What was meaningful about the project? Would they serve there again? What else would they like to do?

The "Serving from Your Sparks" handout/quiz on page 138 helps youth make connections between sparks and service. See if they can find matches between the two columns, matching sparks with service projects. As they make a match, ask them to share how that spark can be used in the service project example. Ask, too, what other sparks can be utilized within that same project.

Note: Many of the service projects can match multiple sparks, so there is no singularly correct answer. Here is one way we matched the projects with sparks: 1. C; 2. G; 3. F; 4. H; 5. B; 6. A; 7. J; 8. I; 9. D; 10. E.

Remind young people that identifying their sparks, priorities, and values can give them a sense of power. Sparks can give young people a compass to guide their lives. How they express sparks is up to them. Only they can decide if they express sparks through art, science, vocation, relationships, or personal time. The point is, they get to explore and be true to themselves.

Serving from Your Sparks · · · · · · · · · · · ·

1. Animal welfare	A. Welcome refugees to town and show them your favorite family activities.
2. Athletics	B. Teach conflict resolution skills to children.
3. Creative arts	C. Publicize pets for adoption at an animal shelter.
4. Helping, caring	D. Play word games, such as Boggle and Scrabble, with children to encourage literacy skills.
5. Leading	E. Lead a meditation class before or after school.
6. Learning (e.g., languages, sciences, history)	F. Lead a character-building puppet show for children.
7. Living a quality life (e.g., joy, tolerance, caring)	G. Help Special Olympics host an athletic event for people with disabilities.
8. Nature, ecology, environment	H. Cook or make sack lunches for a homeless shelter.
9. Reading	I. Build and maintain a community garden and donate the proceeds to a homeless mission.
10. Spirituality, religion	J. Build a wheelchair ramp for an older adult who needs one.

Keepers. . . . .

What do you want to remember from this chapter? What might you use or try? Flip back through the chapter and skim for possibilities or keepers. Record the ideas that intrigue you, seem possible, or make you excited.

. . . .

FOR YOUR BOOKSHELF

Sparks: How Parents Can Help Ignite the Hidden Strengths of Teenagers, by Peter Benson (Jossey-Bass, 2003).

Spark Student Motivation: 101 Easy Activities for Cooperative Learning, by Jolene L. Roehlkepartain (Search Institute Press, 2012).

"Sparks: A Gateway to Developmental Relationships," Search Institute, www.search-institute.org/sparks/about.

Interfaith Youth Corps, www.ifyc.org.

Volunteer Guide, www.volunteerguide.org/.

Change.org, www.change.org.

Idealist, www.idealist.org/info/volunteer/online.

Youth Heroes youtube channel. See videos of youth changing the world. http://bit.ly/1thSvDh.

Work Ethic Scholarships, www.profoundlydisconnected.com.

Stretch Them

In the late 1970s, there were two teenage superheroes known as the Wonder Twins. The twins activated their powers by bumping knuckles and yelling, "Wonder Twin powers activate!" Jayna, the sister, would then say "Shape of a . . ." and announce the animal shape she was going to take—be it a gopher, octopus, or some mythical creature. Then Zan, the brother, would say, "Form of a . . ." and announce the form of water—solid, liquid, or gas—that he would transform into, such as an ice unicycle, a water spout, or an ice cage. Once their powers were activated, they went to work to save the day. And if they ever needed help, they called on their "Super Friends."

What we love about the Wonder Twins is their confidence and their evident problem-solving skills. They didn't falter on what shape or form to take. They had assessed the situation ahead of time, critically analyzed what was going on, and decisively determined the best way to use their powers in any given tough situation. They had experience and confidence, they weren't afraid to take risks to make things right, and they knew that their powers could be channeled in multiple creative ways.

The first step in activating young people's powers—their sense of purpose, sparks, energies, and skills—is to help them explore the world and develop a base of understanding. Before a challenge can be accepted and a problem solved, youth must assess the situation to gain understanding and perspective. They must explore, experience, and learn before they can more fully activate their powers. As they experience and learn, they can begin to test their powers and stretch themselves. This chapter provides ways to begin to develop those budding powers.

Expand Their Perspective

As you spend time with the young people in your group, it's important to maximize opportunities to help them expand their world. Experiencing new people and places, and being introduced to issues around the world puts them on a pathway of discovery. You want to enlarge their experiences and vary them in as many ways as possible. As they engage with the community and the world, they are learning. They are learning about what the problems are, where the pain points exist, and where the opportunities are to further explore their sparks, learn new skills, make friends, and make a difference. They are learning about other people and what makes the community unique. You might introduce them to a foreign food, a different cultural tradition, or a new part of your city; the possibilities are endless—and exciting. You know your youth—their interests, their sparks, and their dreams. Use that information to plan conversations, adventures, activities, and opportunities that will open their eyes and broaden their worldview.

Here are some pathways that you can take to help your youth expand their perspective, learn, and stretch.

Explore the World through Field Trips

Field trips are a powerful way to help youth expand their perspectives. They help youth learn more about the community and expand their horizons of opportunity and awareness. Field trips can reinforce academic, civic, or cultural learning and connect to the personal sparks or interests of young people. Field trips are powerful ways to help youth explore potential connections to the community with regard to internships, career fields, hobbies, and volunteer opportunities.

Choose field trips that give youth different perspectives of what makes the community work and demonstrate a variety of sparks. Try one of these: airport, bakery, pro sports team practice, cathedral, farm, factory, science lab, or military base. Think about what makes your community unique and take youth to explore your community on a deeper level. Where could you take your youth to give them the most diverse perspective possible?

Sparky Places in My World: .... An Activity to Activate Powers

Create an activity exploration list to introduce your youth to different opportunities and places in the community. Ask them where they'd like to go. You can start with the ideas below or add your own from the sparks list at www.search-institute.org/sparks/about. As you stretch them to come up with ideas for what to do, watch for spark connections—those moments when youth get really engaged and excited. Follow up on those moments and help them think about how they can further explore those activities.

After you've completed an activity, check it off. Note any youth who really seemed to enjoy the event and ask them about their experiences to help them further think about their interests. Why did they enjoy it? What was it in particular that they enjoyed? Would they do it again? What else would they like to do?

Activity	Done It?	Notes
Went to an art museum (in person or via the Internet)		
Listened to a concert on YouTube		
Read or heard poetry		
Worked as volunteers at a marathon		
Learned how to cook		
Organized a fund-raiser		
Went to a science museum		
Went to a cultural fair		
Took an art class		

Activity	Done It?	Notes
Went swimming		
Made a YouTube video		
Created a photo collage		
Served at a homeless mission		
Attended a play		
Taught a game to younger children		
Made a bike from parts		
Learned how to interview others		
Rapped		
Learned a dance from another country		
Learned how to manage a 1,400-pound steer		
Decorated a cake		
Sewed clothing or other item		
Learned to shoot archery		

Explore the World through Technology

Technology offers so many ways for youth to connect with others, learn about issues that are important to them, and educate others about their concerns.

STRATEGIC MOVES

- *Use Skype to interact with people around the world. Skyping can prepare youth for what they might experience on an upcoming trip to another part of the world, or it can be a conduit for creating updated versions of "pen pals."*

- *Use virtual classrooms as a venue for your group to connect through technology for the sake of discussions or doing presentations.*
- *Take virtual field trips around the world to learn about any topic. The website www.meetmeatthecorner.org has many virtual field trips submitted by children around the world.*
- *Have youth create and submit their own videos to share on Meet Me at the Corner's website.*
- *Use a search engine to research topics of interest to your group. Just remember to preview any media content that you share with your group.*

EXPANDING YOUTH POWER If a young person enjoys writing, invite him or her to write articles about your program or youth heroes for a blog, a newsletter, or your website. If someone enjoys singing or playing an instrument, see if he or she wants to create a YouTube tutorial. If a youth enjoys organizing, ask if he or she wants to help create a virtual fundraiser or social media campaign.

Explore the World through Careers

The best career advice given to the young is "find out what you like doing best and get someone to pay you for doing it."

Katharine Whitehorn, writer

Show young people possibilities of careers that might fit their interests, passions, and aptitudes. Help them see the possibilities that their lives can take when they identify something they might like to do, work hard, work smart, and follow their heart toward a future they desire. The payoff can impact a child's life. Connect them to caring adults who work in their fields of interest. Introduce them to role models who share their interests to show

how you *can* live out your life from sparky places—those places that bring you deep joy and give meaning to your life. Be a *possibilitarian* for them and show them all the places they can go, do, and be.

Workforce development professional Ellen Zinkiewicz says, "When a young person sees himself as someone with a future with many different possibilities, it will change his outlook on life. Seeing that future encourages positive decision-making because the youth can better see [and understand] that poor decisions might impact that future."

EXPANDING **Encourage job shadowing opportunities**
YOUTH **POWER** **face-to-face or using technology such as YouTube, Skype, or FaceTime to build relationships in cyberspace. Fred Frazier Jr., a youth career coach, suggests these potential allies: local or state government, nonprofit agencies, local businesses, sports clubs, schools, and faith-based communities. Youth should also consider their own network of family, friends, teachers, professors, and coaches.**

STRATEGIC

MOVES

- *Invite youth to create a list of jobs they think might be interesting.*
- *Ask youth to look online for three websites or blogs connected to their career interests and record one exciting fact about the career that appeals to them.*
- *Watch TED lecture videos related to your group's interests.*
- *Give them a career interest inventory, such as this one: www.mynextmove.org/explore/ip (best for youth ages 16 and older).*
- *Help them explore career and college possibilities, using a site like https://bigfuture.collegeboard.org/explore-careers.*

Explore the World Face-to-Face

Truth be told, *nothing* beats face-to-face learning. The best way to learn more about others and broaden our understanding and perspective is to make all kinds of friends. These connections include friends from different backgrounds, religions, and interests. These friends may live on the other side of the globe or the other side of the street. Friends add a heart connection to our lives and make what we learn from them and about them stick. We're better; we're *more* because of our relationships. That's why learning from relationships can be so influential. As our youth explore and get to know how large the world is around them and look at it from others' eyes, their friends' eyes, the possibilities for a new world forged of friendship can emerge. These perspectives create attitudes where a world of peace is possible and bridged by friendship.

Have you considered how you can create face-to-face encounters to explore the world? If your sports team does cross-training, invite an international group to join yours for practice. You can build relationships at the same time that you are working on fitness and training. If your troop is going camping, invite a Special Olympics troop to come along. Teach each other. Laugh together. Make friends.

EXPANDING YOUTH POWER Start an exchange by having your club become pen pals with a group in another country. Use writing to share and learn cultural traditions, spiritual practices, educational opportunities, and geographical features. Or, serve together with another group. If you work with a faith-based group, join up with a different religious group to work together on a service project. Share stories from your various faith traditions of why serving others is important.

One thing I've learned from cross-cultural settings is that "the way" something is done is often just one way to do things, and other people's way of doing something can be just as valid and is not wrong just because it doesn't match our cultural "way" of doing it.

—Melanie Jones, former international development worker, Africa

EXPANDING YOUTH POWER Ask your students when they've been pleasantly surprised that someone became their friend. Where did they first meet? How did the friendships happen? Challenge your group to deliberately seek out and make friends with someone they consider "different" from themselves and whom they would not normally choose to reach out to. It might be a neighbor or someone at school. Come up with two to three questions to ask to help get the conversations going and then invite them to reach out in friendship.

Explore the World through Project-Based Activities

Projects are often a part of curricular and after-school experiences that involve crafts, building kits, and science experiments. Why not use various crafts and projects to deepen exploration of the world and how it works? Grow plants from seedlings and explore the various foods that grow in different areas and climates. Create meals in a kitchen and explore staple foods of different cultures. What is a main dish for dinner in China? Egypt? Sweden?

Build birdhouses and do an online search of backyard birds and birds from different countries and explore migration habits of a particular species. See how we're connected by the things we do and what we need. We live in a globally connected world, and projects done together can be a great way to explore different approaches to commonalities and everyday life.

 Challenge your group to create a compilation of songs, favorite desserts, or stories from around the world (including their own). Challenge them to do the research, collecting, and sharing of the information. Use technology to share what they've learned.

 It is so important for young people to invest time in discovering who they really are and gain perspective about the world around them. Challenge each young person to expand their horizons and see the possibilities around them.

Where would you like to start stretching your youth?

Expand Their Perspective Forward

As you work to help youth develop a base of understanding about the world and themselves, you can challenge them to stretch themselves to picture who they might be in the future—the kind of person they want to be, the values and mission they want to uphold, and the vision they want to live out for their lives. These personal development activities help youth to think about these things.

Nancy Reece, a coach and leadership consultant, created a quiz to help people examine how they are spending their time and to see whether their time is being spent in fulfilling and meaningful ways. We've used this helpful tool many times with others and for ourselves.

The Prioritization Quiz— . . . .
Recognizing What Counts

Do you want to figure out what is truly important in your life? These steps will help you take a good look at how you spend your time.

1. List all the activities you have on your calendar for the month.
2. As you consider each listed activity by itself, ask yourself three questions:
    * How would you feel if this **was the only thing** in your life?
    * How would you feel if this **wasn't** in your life?
    * **Why** are you doing this?

Here are three activities from a young person's schedule and her responses (in *italics*) to show you how this works:

A – *Serving as treasurer for my service club*
    * How would I feel if this was the only thing in my life?
    Empty. I love the service club, but I hate the treasurer part.
    * How would I feel if this wasn't in my life?
    Great because being in charge of all the money is stressful!
    * Why am I doing it? *I said yes because no one else would.*
B – *Writing a column for the school newspaper*
    * How would I feel if this was the only thing in my life?
    Great—I'd love to pursue a writing career.
    * How would I feel if this wasn't in my life?
    Sad; I really enjoy writing.
    * Why am I doing it? *For the challenge and because I enjoy it.*

C – *Playing on the soccer team*

- How would I feel if this was the only thing in my life?
  Not good; I don't really like soccer!
- How would I feel if this wasn't in my life?
  Great—I find myself stressing over it.
- Why am I doing it? *To spend time with my dad who coaches the team.*

Results (decisions I can control):

A – *It's a no-brainer. I should resign as treasurer and enjoy my time as a service club member.*

B – *I need to keep doing this because it makes me happy, and it lets me explore something I might want to do with my life.*

C – *I'll finish the season, resign, and look for other ways to hang out with my dad.*

· ·

Having a sense of your life mission is core; it defines who you are and why you choose to be involved in certain activities. Knowing your purpose and having a sense of mission can make your life fulfilling and satisfying. The trick is to discover your purpose and determine how to stay true to yourself through the ups and downs of life.

Use the "Looking at the Real Me" activity on page 152 to help youth think about what they enjoy doing now and to dream about what they could do in the future. The goal is to give youth another lens to ponder their life mission and begin naming pieces of their life purpose.

Looking at the Real Me . . . .

Ask your youth to take a few minutes to fill in the blanks for some of these statements; they don't have to answer them all.

I am . . .

I do . . .

I believe . . .

I focus . . .

I help . . .

I make . . .

I try . . .

I say . . .

I celebrate . . .

I will . . .

Challenge each person to pick one statement that most resonates with his or her purpose in life. Which statement truly fits with the idea of "do what you love, love what you do"? Have each person write that statement on a piece of canvas, tile, or paper that can be taken home. Ask each person to share this statement with the group.

. . . .

Values Driver's License

Review these values and circle nine that are important to you. Choose the one value that is most important. Write that word in your Values ID Box.

Achievement	Security
Friendships	Knowledge
Pleasure	Self-Respect
Adventure	Leadership
Family	Loyalty
Power and Authority	Stability
Love	Effectiveness
Helping Others	Meaning and Purpose
Freedom	Excellence
Peace	Wealth
Respect	Personal Development
Competence	Wisdom
Integrity	Fame
Faith	Joy
Reputation	Other: _____
Responsibility	Other: _____

VALUES ID

Name: _____

#1 Value: _____

Drivers have to be mindful of road signs and traffic and adjust their driving accordingly. Likewise, values help us determine when it's safe or wise to move forward. Values also signal us to stop or proceed cautiously in an activity that conflicts with our values. Be mindful of your values so your life decisions are made from a place of personal integrity.

Following are some discussion questions for the Values Driver's License exercise:

How did you pick your list of values?

How hard was it to pick one overarching value for yourself?

Which value did you pick? How did you determine "the one"?

How does knowing your core values help you make decisions?

Talk about a time when you've "yielded." A time your values signaled you to "stop." What happened in each situation?

ACTIVITY

Visualizing . . . .

The following visualization exercise is shared by Sharon Williams, a seasoned youth services professional. Have each person take a colored index card. Invite them to close their eyes and visualize what they want to happen in the next year. Ask them to write down what they'd like to accomplish in one year (write the date) with three bulleted goals or hopes. If they struggle to come up with what they want to do, prompt them with questions, such as: What do you want to accomplish in school? In your family? With friends? For your health?

3/30/13

By 3/30/14, I would like to accomplish…
- have a job after school at the vet's clinic
- have a cat
- visit Ireland

Once they have written down their plans, tell them to fold the card and keep it in their binder or wallet where they'll be easily reminded to reread their goals. Challenge your class or group to look at their vision every birthday. They should then reflect on how they've done. Most youth will find they have accomplished some dreams, while other plans fell off the radar or were replaced by other things. The "aha" moments come when youth realize they can set goals for as many things as they want; just because they don't accomplish everything doesn't mean they are unsuccessful. It means their goals changed—and that is perfectly normal and commendable.

. . . .

Creating a Mission Statement

If you want your youth to get to their final destinations, they first need a roadmap. Help them carve out time for personal reflection so they can write a personal mission statement to help them navigate life. In one or two simple sentences, have each person tell the world what they are really about. Their statement should inspire them, connect to a bigger picture of who they are, and indicate how they can improve the world.

Creating a Mission Statement:
Sketch It Out

Sketch out some thoughts about what your personal mission statement might look like. If you need a starting place, complete these statements:

At my core, I am . . . (an encourager, a helper, an entrepreneur)

My mission in life is to . . . (teach, create, write, inspire others to be their best)

Sample mission statement:

I want to live in a way that lets me use my creative energy.
I like to cook and do artwork, and I want to do these things
in ways that include my friends and family.

Your ideas for a mission statement:

Keepers . . . .

What do you want to remember from this chapter? What might you use or try? Flip back through the chapter and skim for possibilities or keepers. Record the ideas that intrigue you, seem possible, or make you excited.

FOR YOUR BOOKSHELF

The 7 Habits of Highly Effective Teens: The Ultimate Teenage Success Guide, by Sean Covey (Fireside, 1998).

Dream boards, a strategy for making a collage that captures your dreams and inspirations. See www.oprah.com/spirit/O-Dream-Board-Envision-Your-Best-LifeTM or www.wikihow.com/Make-a-Dream-Board.

Challenge Them

> [The world's hope] is to rely on youth . . . not a time of life but a
> state of mind, a temper of the will, a quality of the imagination,
> a predominance of courage over timidity, of the appetite for adven-
> ture over the love of ease.
>
> —U.S. Senator Robert F. Kennedy, 1966

In chapter 9 we looked at activating powers by exploring, experiencing, and learning. But it doesn't stop there. Youth must also test their skills, abilities, and guiding values to find their voice and power. They must practice, learn, evaluate, adjust, and try out their theories, beliefs, and solutions again in order to meet and face life's challenges. How can we help? By offering challenge.

First, we need to recognize youth as resources. We need to harness the energies, perspectives, gifts, and understandings of youth *today* as actors and contributors in finding solutions for the challenges in our world. By asking them what they think and asking them to get involved, to help, and to share their gifts, we challenge them to tap into their powers and use them for good. The school of thought that says "Prepare today's youth to become tomorrow's leaders" is rather shortsighted. Steve Culbertson, president and CEO of Youth Service America, actively works with youth leaders, and this is why he does it:

1. Kids don't see borders today the way we did growing up, and they know that problems don't have passports. Half of the world's population is under the age of 25. Youth rule. Sixty percent of

the world's population is under age 30; 50 percent is under age 25; and 40 percent is under age 18. We need to cash the youth dividend and harness their perspective.

2. Young people bring unique skills to solving problems—they bring energy, commitment, idealism, and creativity that adults don't have.

3. There are biological things going on here: Between the ages of 12 and 25, there are three big drivers happening in every adolescent brain:

    *   **Novelty**—youth crave novelty. What that does is bring new solutions to problems. We're not going to change biology, so let's tap into that and try something new.

    *   **Risk**—young people take more risks than older people do. "No risk, no reward." We need that risk. It's what moves society forward; we need to take risks and experiment with solutions to the big problems facing us. Young people will take risks that adults, organizations, and governments can't afford to take for fear of failure.

    *   **Peer authority (or peer pressure)** is a big drive during the adolescent years. Peer pressure can be a positive thing. Young people check out what other youth are doing. Youth can create a movement. They can create a tipping point where young people encourage other young people to help them tackle the big social issues facing them.

We need to take advantage of these gifts of youth. The problems before us are so big today. We can't afford to wait until young people are grown up before they understand the problems, learn about them, find their voice, take action, and have an impact. And many of the problems involve youth, including childhood obesity or the fact that one in four youth go hungry. We need to turn the problem over to them and ask them to be the solvers of it. This is a powerful strategy that works.

History has shown that youth can be powerful forces, working as advocates and raising awareness about big issues—they were part of the seatbelt movement, the anti-littering movement, the smoking cessation movement, and the recycling movement. All of these were driven by youth.

Steve challenges us all to "Ask them to do good. Ask them to make the world a better place." As youth leaders, your purpose is to challenge youth *now*—to engage them and their hearts, insights, experiences, and energies in creating solutions to complex problems and to help them realize for themselves that they have the power to make a difference.

Stepping Up to Meet Challenges

The point is not to become a leader. The point is to become yourself, to use yourself completely—all your skills, gifts, and energies—in order to make our vision manifest. You must withhold nothing. You must, in sum, become the person you started out to be, and to enjoy the process of becoming.

—Warren Bennis, author

Imagine your youth as self-directed, self-confident, able to manage their emotions and selves, responsible, sensitive to others, aware of the world, and working to meet needs. Imagine their eyes opening wide with realization as they recognize their gifts and sense of purpose. Wow! Put that together with their natural energy, love of novelty, and willingness to challenge the status quo, and you change the world!

You have the honor of creating spaces and places for youth to put into motion the ideas, actions, and influence that they hope to have. In your program, they become ready for life; they connect what they are learning and experiencing to their personal identities. As you provide opportunities for them to apply ideas and skills, express themselves, and engage as influencers in the world, they begin to learn how to act in meaningful ways to become more fully themselves.

Here we offer ideas on how you can challenge youth to put their ideas, values, and actions to work.

Challenge Them to Think, Solve, and Do

Everyone benefits from having the ability to think for themselves and to come up with solutions to problems, whether big or small, complex or mundane. Young people need to know how to identify challenges—and that includes recognizing what the "real" issue is within a challenge. Young people must also be allowed to think creatively to meet and solve challenges. This capacity for critical thinking is so important that the Partnership for 21st Century Skills (P21) has identified it as a key skill students need in order to be prepared for learning, the workplace, and life.

Some of our young people reach high school age and don't yet see themselves as leaders. And yet, as Steve Culbertson so articulately outlined, youth have the prime capacity to bring fresh eyes, ideas, and out-of-the-box thinking to confront complex world issues. Dance instructor Patricia Cross says, "Children are capable of much more than we expect of them, and they want to be challenged." Usually, the problem isn't that youth haven't taken action but that we have failed to challenge kids to step up to opportunities to serve, lead, and help. A creative and enlightening way to challenge youth is through project-based learning.

Challenging Youth to Solve Problems

Young people are so bright and often their brains are not fettered by the critical spirit that squashes the creative abilities of adults. Adults have often been told too many times that their ideas won't work or that systems are too hard to change. But most youth haven't heard that message repeatedly, so they seem to have more freedom to tackle problems with enthusiasm and courage.

Project-based learning engages youth in learning as they grapple with real-world problems and challenges, and work collaboratively to develop solutions that will stimulate improvements. So instead of just studying climate change, youth are given an open-ended question about the problems related to climate change and are challenged to answer it together. Questioning and applying critical thinking are relevant strategies used by youth as they research, compile data, develop plans for change, and present it in a compelling manner. Project-based learning offers opportunities in the classroom for youth to identify problems and then focus on solving them during the course of the class.

Odyssey of the Mind and Destination Imagination are two national organizations that offer creative problem-solving challenges through tournaments and competitions. Youth are challenged to work together to solve the problems by tapping into creative thinking skills. These groups tackle everything from building structures to solving mind puzzles, writing scripts, and interpreting literature. Some of their problem solving is done spontaneously in timed competitions (check out Odyssey of the Mind's website for practice problems), whereas others are in the planning and designing stage for months before the competition.

You can also challenge youth in a virtual world, where they can use technology and games as a tool to do good in the world. These games, each in their own way, offer education, understanding, and perspective on different social and world situations. Youth can explore, experience, and learn about complex challenges in our world. They can solve these issues by using their heads. Pick a game to explore from this list: "15 Serious Games Aiming to Change the World" at www.dailygood.org/more.php?n=5209.

Consultant Kelli Walker-Jones says that when it comes to challenging youth you should, "Set something up where the process is more important than the outcome. We're trying to challenge these young people to interact and make the world a better place *today*. And every time an adult facilitates that process (a loving, strength-based process), then the very act of that process makes the world a better place right then because of what's going on in the group—it prepares them to make a better world and at the same time makes the world better in that moment because of *what's happening right then*." She adds, "Prepare to be surprised and let go of all your preconceived notions. I knew how to solve the spontaneous problems [in Odyssey of the Mind], but I was constantly surprised at how they solved them. And their solutions, different from mine, often worked. It's amazing."

STRATEGIC

MOVES

- *Don't make problem solving easy and don't cave in to the desire to give young people all the answers. Let youth struggle with the issue. It's their issue, their problem; they have to solve it.*
- *Get out of the way and focus on process, not outcome.*
- *Try one of the problem solvers from the Odyssey of the Mind website, www.odysseyofthemind.com/practice.*

Letting Go of Expectations

1. What would happen if you didn't anticipate particular outcomes but instead genuinely waited to see what your group would come up with?

2. What would happen if you were invested in the whole process instead of just the results?

3. What can you do to help yourself focus on the process?

Journal Exercise

Challenge Them to Serve

Young people all over the world are serving, helping others in need, and volunteering to make the world a better place by planting, building, sharing food, and doing numerous other acts of kindness. Many youth are also engaged in service-learning, where they are serving others and being intentional about learning from that service. As they are serving, they might be practicing leadership skills, learning about another culture, fine-tuning a sports technique, or practicing their geometry lesson. Service and service-learning are both powerful ways to challenge young people in classrooms, clubs, and after-school settings.

Serving others builds character and moves us away from a naturally self-centered focus. When youth serve, they almost always end up receiving more than they give. Serving others opens their eyes to parts of the world that they have never seen before. They see the underbellies of communities. They see the "invisible" people who live around them. They see the vulnerabilities in hearts. They see the possibilities in people and in neighborhoods. They see unsung heroes and people who come up with amazing solutions to everyday problems. Youth see a whole new world. Service is an opportunity for youth to gain perspective, deepen understanding, interact with different people and situations, examine old beliefs against new data, use critical thinking skills, and take risks to find answers or solutions and make things better.

Service-learning turns into something magical when youth use their gifts to inspire others around them. How can you challenge your group to activate their powers and gifts to serve in the community? Helping others can be as simple as doing acts of kindness or as large as searching for a cure for cancer.

Opportunities to serve are all around you. First, get out in the community to see where other youth and adults are helping others! Pay attention to local media sources, and look for stories about helpful citizens and groups that interest you. You might hear of a group that plays Frisbee with children with special needs, or a group such as Kaboom! that builds playgrounds in

The Power of Service-Learning

Courtney Lawrence, an educator in Japan, says she loves engaging youth in service-learning because they change, claim their power, and realize that they can come up with solutions to human issues and needs. Her challenge with each class is to help her students understand that they don't have to ask for permission to do good. "At 18 and 19, I want them to realize that they can use their heads, eyes, hands, hearts, and ideas to do something to help make situations better. They don't have to ask their parents. They don't have to get permission. They can look, study, try, and do. To see that change in them, to see them begin to understand and take action to make something happen in the world is what it is all about!"

low-income areas, or a group that is teaching a foreign language to young children. Look on the Internet to find lists of nonprofit groups that fit with your interest areas. The United Way is often a great place to start looking for local agencies that serve in the community.

Work side by side with others to improve a situation by building a wheelchair ramp for someone, planting trees at a park, walking dogs at the animal shelter, or raising money for a cause that is important to you. Work a political poll. Help at a blood bank. Clean a stream. Hand out meals. Check to see if you have a community volunteer center or a group that coordinates volunteer opportunities in your city—these groups are like volunteer clubs, where individuals can meet up with others to volunteer in projects that they select, and they can often coordinate service projects for groups.

Another strategy is to start from what youth know and build from there: a book club might want to start a reading club for kids at a homeless shelter; a knitting club could knit caps for cancer patients in a local hospital; and a debate club can advocate for issues they are passionate about. Challenge youth to serve in a way that extends naturally from their interests. Challenge the group to educate the community about a cause that is important to them.

To get your youth motivated to serve, show them examples of young people their age who are doing incredible work in the world. You can use visual tools, such as videos and YouTube clips; or read material from newspapers, blogs, and case studies to encourage youth to observe and learn from other youth. In our Youth Heroes YouTube channel at http://bit.ly/1thSvDh we have collected examples of young people who are meeting and overcoming challenges.

STRATEGIC

MOVES

- *Initiate the Smile Card challenge, where you ask everyone in your program to do an anonymous nice deed for someone and to leave the person with a printed or homemade Smile Card that asks them to pay it forward. For more information, visit www.kindspring.org/ smilecards/.*
- *Determine an issue your group wants to tackle together, apply for a mini-grant (find ideas in For Your Bookshelf), and take on the project.*

For more service ideas, see pages 121–30 in chapter 8 to explore that important connection between serving and sparks.

Challenge Them to Speak Up and Speak Out

Advocacy is a powerful response to seeing community or world needs and taking corrective actions. Youth make powerful advocates on issues that affect them. They are quick to speak up about rules that are unfair, and they know firsthand what they're talking about. On the flip side, if youth aren't speaking up regularly in the program space, then they aren't being prepared to speak up in the advocacy space. Help them practice during your group time.

We once worked with an urban youth group that advocated against predatory lenders who were targeting their families and communities, trapping them in an inescapable cycle of debt. In low-wealth communities, some unscrupulous businesses charged as much as 400 percent interest rates on small, supposedly onetime loans. Our group of youth researched the issue, its impact on their families, the business models where they borrowed from one to pay the other, and the laws that allowed for outlandish interest rates. Armed with knowledge, they stepped up to educate the community about the dangers of quick cash and to investigate how they could change community systems to protect people who are unaware of the dangers. They also partnered with an adult-led citywide neighborhood collaborative to investigate and advocate policy changes for their communities.

> The work of advocacy depends on research, critical thinking, and understanding. The young people in your class or program will need an understanding of who is involved in an issue and impacted by it. They will need to understand who has power in the issue, how they keep this power, and what differing points of view need to be considered. It is important to do a power analysis related to the cause they're interested in. Young people need to understand that many issues are complicated and institutionalized, making change difficult—but not impossible.
>
> —Anderson Williams, entrepreneur,
> artist, and educational consultant

Speaking out can start at any age. Six-year-old children in Turkey educated others on scarcity and water conservation. These children, after researching information on water with older students, dressed up as water droplets and did flash mobs in front of government buildings and malls to bring attention to the issue. They did a water dance and attracted attention. They then educated others on what they learned about scarcity and conservation. "These kids will know for the rest of their lives that they are assets and resources, not victims or problems to be solved," says Steve Culbertson.

Take a Stand

What issues is your group willing to take a stand on? Poll your group by having each person vote with their feet by simultaneously moving to a corner of the room that represents their answer. Group members will be able to look around the room to see the kinds of social issues each person is interested in. This will also help you gauge the interests of your group, so you can know what kinds of service or advocacy projects to explore together.

You have extra money to donate to a cause. Will you give it to help the homeless or to address environmental issues?

You have a day to volunteer. Will you help the animal shelter or a nursing home?

You are going to answer the phone to accept donations for a service group. Would you rather answer the phone for raising money for world hunger or for saving the whales?

You get to choose how the city will spend its financial and physical resources. Will you vote to help disaster relief victims or senior citizens?

You've been chosen to speak to a group of lawmakers. Would you rather speak about childhood obesity or violence in schools?

Ask the group for other causes that mean something to them and why they're important to them. Brainstorm ways youth can help. Then get busy! Pick an issue you want to tackle or a project idea that everyone agrees on and get to work.

EXPANDING YOUTH POWER Social media gives many opportunities for voices to be heard, to "like" campaigns, to sign petitions, to educate through status updates. Challenge your group to create awareness around an issue important to them using social media streams to get the word out.

Challenge Them to Become Social Entrepreneurs

If your young people are fired up about tackling issues and have ideas for wide-scale change, they may be social entrepreneurs in the making. Do your young people seem to be change agents at heart? Do they seek to invent new approaches and improve systems? "That's what social entrepreneurs do," says Bill Drayton, CEO of Ashoka. "Social entrepreneurs are not content just to give a fish or teach how to fish. They will not rest until they have revolutionized the fishing industry." Social entrepreneurs often weave philanthropy and business with ideas that unstick systems or impact communities in big, powerful, society-changing ways.

STRATEGIC

MOVES

- *Invite your youth to take a social entrepreneur quiz or practice building a socially conscious business at the New Heroes, "Are You the Next New Hero?" www.pbs.org/opb/thenewheroes/engage/.*
- *Read stories of other young social entrepreneurs in this article: "Meet the 25 Most Influential People in the World!" Huffington Post, June 18, 2012, www.huffingtonpost.com/ news/25-most-powerful-and-influential-young-people-in-the-world.*
- *As a group, join others in solving big challenges at www.openideo.com/.*
- *Teach a course on social entrepreneurship. Check out the free curriculum at the New Heroes, "Classroom Materials," www.pbs.org/opb/thenewheroes/teachers/.*
- *Find funding for creative projects at Kickstarter, www.kickstarter.com/.*
- *Be inspired by other ideas at http://innovideo.tv/ and at http://changemaking.ashoka.org/.*

TAKE 2 TWO It is so important for young people to put into action their strengths, their styles, and who they really are. Don't let them just follow in the steps of their peers or adults they admire. Challenge them to dig deep, discover what's in their gut, and use their gifts to make a difference in the world.

How would you like to start challenging your youth?

. . . .

📇 FOR YOUR BOOKSHELF

"Framework for 21st Century Learning," Partnership for 21st Century Skills, www.p21.org/our-work/p21-framework.

"Resources," BIE, www.bie.org/resources.

Odyssey of the Mind, www.odysseyofthemind.com.

Destination Imagination, www.destinationimagination.org/.

"Want PBL?" Buck Institute for Education, www.youtube.com/user/BIEPBL.

Do Something, www.dosomething.org.

generationOn, www.generationon.org.

Kids Make It Better: A Write-in, Draw-in Journal, by Suzy Becker (Workman Publishing Company, 2010).

Ready-to-Go Service Projects: 140 Ways for Youth Groups to Lend a Hand, by Susan Ragsdale and Ann Saylor (Abingdon Youth, 2008).

Seasons of Service: Engaging Youth throughout the Year, by Susan Ragsdale and Ann Saylor.

YMCA Center for Asset Development, 2012. Free curriculum available at http://theassetedge.net/seasons-of-service.pdf.

Youth Heroes, http://bit.ly/1thSvDh.

Youth Service America, www.ysa.org.

Power Up

Thus far in the book we've explored what motivates and energizes young people. Is it advocacy? Is it art? It is swimming? Is it rock 'n' roll? Is it working with numbers and calculators? When young people discover their passions, they are on their way to finding their purpose and determining how they can show up in the world. In chapter 1, we noted that the ultimate goal for leaders interested in positive youth development is to expand and share power. This chapter discusses how to intentionally expand youth power. How can your young people begin to walk in their strengths and extend their sense of purpose in the world? How can they use their powers responsibly?

Expression of power differs for each young person. One may take on systems and try to change them to improve lives. Another may be a budding artist who believes in the power of the spoken word. Another will create masterpieces of design. Another will focus on helping individuals realize their power. And yet another may do things big and loud, making waves in advocacy or leading huge initiatives. The possibilities of expression are endless.

Our job is not to force young people into particular pathways of power but to help them tap into, realize, and use their personal power well. The goal is to help young people use their strengths to the best of their abilities. Young people need to be coached to understand how to use their power in ways that nurture it, rather than abuse or squander it. They need to understand how to use their power with intentionality, so they learn how to stand up or speak up for what's just, good, and beautiful in the world.

Power: It's a Two-Way Street

The unexamined life isn't worth living.

—Socrates

Youth are far too accustomed to sitting and absorbing information from adults in a one-way direction. Rarely do adults take the time to truly ask youth what they think or invite them to explore their own ideas for creating or changing agencies, systems, or communities. Young people have the brain power and heart passion to develop great ideas and make amazing things happen, and you, hopefully, have discovered how well they enjoy solving problems. They just need adults to believe in them and invite them to stretch toward their potential. You can create those dynamics. Are you ready? Test your readiness with the "Attitude Check for Adult Leaders" quiz.

EXERCISE

Attitude Check for Adult Leaders . . . .

How ready are you to activate powers? Do you have hidden biases that get in the way? A good way to find out about our attitudes comes from "Tips for Shared Learning among Youth and Adults" by Anderson Williams. We have adapted his tips into an exercise. Check one statement in each pair that *best* describes your attitudes and actions:

A. I come willing and ready to listen and learn.
   I assume that I know more or have more valuable knowledge than the youth.

B. I facilitate everything or am the first to speak.
   I work to make sure a youth is the first to speak.

C. I keep self and other adults in check; I share the airspace.
   I dominate the conversation; I do most of the talking.

D. **I help ensure** a safe environment for all to offer their input and ideas.

I allow the outspoken or more experienced youth to dominate or rule the experience for all.

E. **I assume** that everyone understands why they are here and how they need to be together.

I clearly articulate the roles, responsibilities, and expectations for all youth and adult participants.

F. **I limit** youth voice, engaging them enough to check it off my to-do list.

I articulate from an adult perspective why youth voice is so important.

G. **I set up** youth to feel engaged and valued but then don't follow through by giving them power to take the lead on important issues, during events, or in conversations.

I articulate and ensure the importance of youth power by letting them take the lead on important issues, during events, and in conversations.

H. **I lead** with a question.

I deliver answers.

I. **I see** youth as resources and problem solvers for issues today.

I am helping to prepare youth to be resources and problem solvers for the future.

If you answered A1, B2, C1, D1, E2, F2, G2, H1, and I1, then you are right on target!

. . . .

Dynamite youth workers and educators show up fully attentive and ready to share and learn as part of the team. They create spaces and invitations for youth to speak up, act, and experiment with their powers. They know when to sit quietly, when to ask probing questions, and when to let youth struggle with themselves. And they know when to step back and let youth fly. They are trustworthy and respectful, and they prove themselves over time.

It is here that our commitment to working *with* youth instead of doing *for* youth gets tried and tested, often on a daily basis. This is where I'm forced to decide whether I will plan an event for youth or will support them as they plan. Will I coach them through leading a presentation for the city council, or will I dominate the presentation? These are the moments when we are reminded that our role is to coach, to encourage, to be patient, and to focus on the process instead of the results. Will we expand power by letting young people do for themselves, and will we at the same time offer the opportunities and the encouragement for them to try?

You can be that kind of support. It's not always easy, and it takes practice. You'll need to ask trusted youth and adults about the way you are perceived in a group setting and be willing to humbly accept their feedback. Then you'll need to muster the vision and courage to make necessary shifts in your attitudes and behavior. Never underestimate the power of your attitude and how you've been shaped by experiences for good or for bad. You are a powerful influence. All your experiences, perspectives, and even prejudices show. Sometimes, we're not aware of how they hinder us.

TAKE TWO

As you think about what's "right on," what do you need to personally do to improve how effectively you engage youth in activating their powers? Pick one of the "right on" ideas to ponder in the space below. Or, consider ways that you can learn from youth, allowing them to teach *you* something.

. . . .

Quiz Blues?

After taking the quiz, are you thinking, *Really? You're asking me to do how much more? It's all on me? Typical. Ask more of the teacher or youth worker.* And you may even imagine youth voices saying, "Yeah, you adults need to do that. Yeah, you need to listen to us. Let us talk."

Fret not. So far, we've only covered the adult side of the equation. That's only half the picture. There's a youth side, and, if you'll indulge us, we'll now address their attitudes and actions. We suggest that you invite your young people to assess themselves. Use the "Attitude Check for Youth" handout on page 178 with your youth to ensure that just as you show up to learn, share, and give, they will also come with an attitude and willingness to contribute to learning and sharing together. After they've taken the quiz, talk about each set of pairs and how this group can be one that shows up in full power. Talk, too, about the quiz you took.

Attitude Check for Youth

How do you show up to this group? Circle one statement in each pair of sentences that best describes you. Be honest! Don't overinflate. This exercise, adapted with permission from "Tips for Shared Learning among Youth and Adults" by Anderson Williams, is intended to help you learn about yourself. You don't need to show it to others.

A. I come willing and ready to contribute ideas, listen, and learn.
    I assume adults won't take me seriously or aren't really interested in hearing the truth from my perspective.

B. I team up with people I know or who share ideas in an attempt to "win" a conversation.
    I encourage everyone in the group to contribute to the process and speak their truth.

C. I defer leadership or expertise to adults.
    I step up and respectfully articulate when I feel an adult is dominating a conversation.

D. I show up just because someone told me to or because I get out of school.
    I bring honesty, energy, and my unique ideas and experiences to the conversation.

E. I respect people with different backgrounds and experiences.
    I assume that everyone has had my same experiences.

F. I leave this program and go home without working to change anything.
    I follow up by taking my ideas and information and putting them to work.

G. I have fun or make things fun!
    I complain about being bored without helping to make things fun.

How Did You Do?

If you answered A1, B2, C2, D2, E1, F2, and G1, then you are rocking and ready to serve and lead in your group! If you answered A2, B1, C1, D1, E2, F1, and G2, then you are in need of a "bump up" in attitude, expectations, and hopes. It's time you tap into your power and beliefs to put them to work for good. If you found yourself somewhere in between, that's okay. Becoming aware of what we need to work on helps us identify how we can be more in tune with our power.

As you can see from the two quizzes, it takes two sides to complete the picture. Talk about this with your youth. It's not just about asking adults to do more. If the only thing youth are asking is for adults to do more, then youth are continuing to defer their power to adults. Youth have work to do, too. This is about both sides doing things differently and taking responsibility for the results.

Getting Strategic:
Framing How Power Can Look for Your Program

Our goal throughout this book has been to provide you with examples, strategies, and ideas for shaping your program and interactions from a strength-based mind-set. We've done that in order to meet our ultimate goals around youth development:

- Build on the internal strengths and capacities of young people
- Help young people know their sparks and have a sense of purpose
- Help young people discover their power and learn to use their power well

As you read through the first part of this chapter, you have probably had some positive thoughts—*I like that idea!*—and some doubts—*You want me to do what?* Let's pause here to address the realities of the structures of your workplace. We want to provide an opportunity for you to put into context how "powering up" might actually look in your program or classroom. First, we need to emphasize that *no two programs are alike, and no two programs will use the same formula for helping youth "power up."*

Some programs offer "meet ups"—events where all the young people are invited to come out and participate. These types of events connect people around common interests. In these cases, there may not be much infrastructure for helping youth "power up." And that's fine. These programs offer youth the chance to choose what they want to participate in and can be the incubator where they discover their heartbeat. That discovery may lead them to decide where to go to further develop their skills or explore interests. This is an important contribution to expanding power: the identification of passions and interests.

Other programs have a set "power design" where the involvement of youth requires a larger commitment of time and contribution. Volleyball leagues, for example, are all about developing volleyball skills, along with deeper elements of collaboration, communication, and leadership through leading drills, being captain, and so forth. Bands and choirs practice together and independently, often under youth leadership through sections and solos, in order to improve musical techniques and learn to perform together. Youth Congress members know that they will work on core skills related to passing congressional bills, and youth will use their power to research, lobby, and present their ideas in small groups and large forums. These programs offer a different kind of space than "meet ups" offer and provide more opportunity for the adult coach to expand the function of power in the group. Hopefully, you're catching on to the fact that there is an involvement function of power: The more opportunities your program offers for youth to be involved and step into taking on tasks and leadership roles, the more you *expand* power.

Where Will I Start? How Much Can I Do?

Your first challenge is to think about what your program's intention is and then, based on your answer, determine how your program can realistically evolve into helping youth discover their passions, purpose, and power. Assessing your program will help you get clear about what you offer and where you can and want to "power up." It will also help you be clear and honest in presenting your program to youth—what it is about, what they can expect from the experience, and what the opportunities are. It eliminates any erring sense of enthusiasm to be all things to all young people. In being real, you put the choice into their hands—they can decide whether your program is the right one for them.

In order to be that articulate and knowledgeable about your program, it's important for you to understand where *you* are right now. It's important for you to self-assess, to identify where you are, and then to think about where you want to be, and how much you want to expand efforts and power. As you self-assess, be as honest as possible. Keep thinking about what you've learned regarding the importance of building strengths and power. What are you willing to do? And by that we mean, what are you *really* willing to do, day in and day out, in your program?

Self-assessment involves the following:

- Identify where you already expand power (and celebrate what you already do!).
- Ask yourself—and be brutally honest—about how much power you are willing and able to share.
- Think about how you can, to the best of your abilities, expand power. Identify where you want to be as a program, classroom, and leader.
- Assess your plan: How much support can you expect from your agency or school on your quest to give youth power?

Here's a visual to give perspective to the assessment: Picture yourself standing over a pond. Toss a pebble into the water. Does it go straight to the bottom, creating a deep reach? Or does it have a light touch that nevertheless sends waves across a great expanse of the water? Notice the circular ripples and waves that gently spread out from that intentional act. Notice how wide the circles expand, how far out they extend before things become calm again. Your program creates ripples. Your actions generate power and expand power. Let's figure out how much you can expand power in youth right now. Then let's determine how much and how far you want to extend and widen your powerful surge.

So, get started. Use the following worksheets to honestly assess what's possible and has promising potential.

Ripples of Power: . . . .
Where Are You Expanding Power?

This exercise is adapted from Anderson Williams's "Understanding the Continuum of Youth Involvement." Read each circle (ripple) individually. Place a checkmark next to one choice in each ripple to indicate the action that you most often take in engaging youth power. Celebrate the ways you are already sharing power.

Youth Roles

Youth are involved in the "doing" of the activity but not in the planning, development, or reflection.

Youth are part of conversations regarding planning and implementing ideas. Their input is considered, but they may or may not have an official "vote."

Youth are involved at all levels of idea or project development and have formal and informal leadership roles in the process.

Youth are the primary drivers of the work, from conceptualization to implementation to reflection. Youth "own" and understand the work deeply.

Adult Roles

Adults develop, plan, and organize all aspects of the activity or event that a cadre of young people will actually carry out.

Adults develop and set the agenda and facilitate the process. Adults include the input of youth in this process through focus groups, meetings, or formal votes.

Adults are involved in the full process and support the development of individual youth and the flow of the process but balance power and leadership with youth. Adults allow youth to struggle and make mistakes in a safe environment.

Adults provide a support role and share ownership and commitment but with some deference to the youth. Adults hold one "vote" on the team.

Decision Making

Adults make all decisions.

Adults ultimately make the decision with the consideration of youth input. If youth have a vote, they are typically outnumbered or adults have ultimate veto power.

Youth and adults share decision-making power, often requiring a specific and mutually agreed upon decision-making process.

Youth ultimately make the decisions with the inclusion of adult input and "vote."

Accountability

Adults are accountable for all aspects of what's going on, including whether or not young people are present. Youth have some secondary accountability to participate in the activity.

Adults maintain accountability for decision making and actions. Youth may have specific accountability for smaller roles and activities that involve youth specifically.

Youth and adults share accountability at all levels of the work.

Youth have primary accountability at all levels of the work. Adults have secondary accountability for ensuring that youth are prepared and supported in a way that they can achieve success.

Read back through each ripple and consider how you might want to expand power. Think about changes you may be able to create in your program and star the choice that best represents where you can realistically expand power. These are the descriptors of ripple impact that you want to thoughtfully put into action to "bump up" your work. There is a time and space for each ripple. No two programs are alike so the impact of your work is uniquely yours and based on what your program is designed to do and how you want to expand power, given what you now know about the importance of sharing power with youth.

After identifying your aspirations for the program, create an action plan to make that statement become a truth about your program, one you can articulate clearly when you tell youth about your program and the opportunities they can expect within it. Remember to include a plan for getting the administrative and community support you need to make your dream become a reality.

EXERCISE

Reflecting on Your Early Roles . . . .

Recalling how you were engaged as a youth might give you some perspective on what it means to share power. For this exercise, you will need a red and a blue pen. Look at the following list of leadership power opportunities. If you were involved in one of these roles as a young person, circle the activity with a red pen.

Architectural design committee	Researcher	Presenter
Committee member	Advisory board member	Teacher
Coach	Workshop facilitator	Panelist
Repairer	Peer mediator	Mentor
Activity leader	Petitioner	Recruiter
Babysitter	Tutor	Surveyor
Producer	Director	Writer
Analyzer	Planner	Editor
Evaluator	Host	Publicist
Judge	Volunteer	Tour guide
Coordinator	Writer	Grant writer
Other: _____	Other: _____	

Use the grid above to think about how you currently engage youth. With the blue pen, circle any roles you have delegated to a young person. Then take time to reflect on the correlation between the two lists and where you might consider sharing power with a young person.

EXERCISE

Engaging Youth Power. . . . .

List the last three projects and initiatives you did with your youth group or classroom.

1.

2.

3.

Who led those projects and initiatives? Mark a **Y** for youth, **A** for adults, or **S** for shared leadership next to each one.

Write down an upcoming project: _____

How can you start to expand power to put youth in charge? List various ways that you can involve youth in leadership roles:

1.

2.

3.

Which of your youth are ready to step up and lead? How can you use their strengths in various roles?

Young Person's Name	Strengths They Have	Potential Leadership Roles

Dig deeper: Which youth might be a hindrance in your program? How might you invite them to use their strengths in leadership?

1.

2.

3.

What training would potential youth leaders need to be successful?

Power-Up Ideas

Following are more ways to help you power up your youth.

Nudge youth who are hesitant to take on leadership roles. Start by encouraging youth to share their sparks. When caught up in the passion of a spark, youth tend to have a boost of confidence and are less self-conscious. Then help them find ways to use their sparks to serve and lead in your program. They will become a coach, an expert, or a mentor without even realizing they were stepping into a leadership position.

Start small. Start sharing power by delegating smaller tasks, such as serving snacks, organizing workspaces, decorating the building, or helping with a fund-raiser. Then progress to more complex tasks, such as reading to preschool children, leading games for younger children, helping peers with homework, being an assistant coach for a children's soccer team, or being a buddy for a newcomer in your program.

Look for ways to spotlight youth strengths during program time. Let them tell jokes, lead activities, demonstrate martial arts or another skill, or cook for parent night. As they explore and live by their sparks, you will see youth come alive, and you will witness a new spirit of life in your group. The ramifications of that new spirit are endless.

Let the Power Flow

> Every action you take is an expression of the choice you have
> made about the effect you want to have on the world.
> —Constance Dembrowsky, speaker and educational consultant

Now that you have some strategies for how to frame your program so that youth can share the power, the work is, in some measure, just beginning. You will need to continue to look for ways to expand power in your group by sharing responsibilities for tasks and leadership. Throughout the book, we have shared ways you can generate power and provide practice opportunities for youth to walk in their power. We thought this might be a good place to remind you of some of those daily disciplines. Remember to create the space for your youth to do the following:

Make choices
Make decisions
Allocate priorities
Determine activities
Influence topics
Set and uphold norms
Take the lead on projects
Advocate

Youth will be more prepared to navigate personal and group choices in the future if you let them take the lead. Let them practice decision making, communication, time management, and leadership. As you plan your schedules, activities, and programming, where can youth take the initiative? Can they help in the following ways?

Call the group to order
Give a thought for the day
Lead the group session
Write a grant for a project
Create a website
Settle a conflict between peers

TAKE TWO

1. Who makes most of the decisions that affect youth in your program—youth or adults?
2. How can you start giving youth more opportunities to make decisions in your program?
3. What young people could you ask for program input?
4. What would you like to know about?
5. How will you let them know that you are listening to their feedback and implementing their ideas?

· ·

Young people, when given the freedom to think and dream, are full of ideas. When you sincerely seek their input, you will begin to understand how much they have to offer. Ask them for ideas for your programming. Ask them how to get more youth involved. Ask them what the community thinks of your program and how to improve that reputation. Ask them how you could grow the program. Once you start asking, be ready for the flow of ideas. Listen and consider the ideas carefully. With the ones that you and your youth want to make happen, remind them that it takes responsibility and work. If they want to host a mini-triathlon, for example, to raise money for a cause and that fits your program's goals, then that's fine—as long as they take on the responsibility for making it happen.

Are You Listening?

If you want young people to *really* talk and voice their opinions, you need to listen twice as much as you speak. Never ask for youth input if you don't intend to truly use their ideas. Disregarding young people's feedback is one of the best ways to ensure that youth won't contribute to your planning.

Helping young people walk in their power takes flexibility on your part, but the results are worth it. As you continue to let the program evolve to reflect their worlds and ideas, they will grow to fiercely protect and advocate for the program. When you consistently look for ways to let them shine and contribute from a place of strength and sparks, and when you practice that mind-set until it becomes as natural as breathing, you will change the fabric of your classroom or organization by infusing it with creativity, hope, challenge, and vitality.

Expanding the Ripples to Other Adults

One important way youth leaders can advocate for youth is to expand the ripples, so to speak, with peers and other adults. When you take on the role of challenging adults and organizations to think more intentionally about youth participation, you expand opportunities for youth power and involvement. On an individual level, speak to the youth leaders around you. Notice them, help them to notice their strengths, invite them to walk in their power, and encourage their efforts. If an adult assumes what youth want or need, encourage him or her to ask youth directly. If an adult is making a decision regarding young people, ask whether he or she has engaged youth in the decision-making process. If there is a community board or committee of adults that influences youth life (such as the city council, mayor's office,

4-H, Scouts, YMCA, or United Way), ask whether two or three youth can join the board. If you are invited to a community meeting, ask if you can bring an interested young person with you. Keep pushing the envelope to help youth gain a platform for expressing their thoughts and ideas.

On a larger scale, take time to share your stories about youth walking in their power and doing good things in the community. Negative stories tend to dominate the media. The good stories too often get lost in the muddle. When you see a young person or a group of young people doing something good, speak up. Tell them directly. Brag to others. Send an e-mail to your favorite television station. Call your favorite radio station. Post it via social media. Tell the story to a friend.

Other adults might get uncomfortable when they see you giving youth power. Be sure to educate your colleagues, peers, and parents about your goals and strategies. Help them understand what you are trying to do in your classroom or program. Explain your philosophy and the environment for youth engagement that you are trying to create. Spell it out and ask them to support your work.

 Keepers . . . .

What do you want to remember from this chapter? What might you use or try? Flip back through the chapter and skim for possibilities or keepers. Record the ideas that intrigue you, seem possible, or make you excited.

. . . .

FOR YOUR BOOKSHELF

Empowering Youth: How to Encourage Young Leaders to Do Great Things, by Kelly Curtis (Search Institute Press, 2008).

PART THREE:
Sustaining Power

The Practice of Self-Mastery

Chapter 12

Part 3 is for you. In the next three chapters, we explore how *you* can sustain personal power for life. We continue to speak to concepts and strategies that you can share and teach your youth, but we pay close attention to you, too. You are the role model and path shaper for youth. You have chosen the precious work of developing youth as your career. You have one of the most vital roles that anyone could ever play in the community, and we believe that it's important that you care for yourself and practice sustaining power so that you can continue to work with youth every day from a place of strength. We start by exploring ways to sustain power by learning how to develop self-mastery of emotions.

The Art of Managing Emotions

Emotions are a powerful force, especially during the adolescent years when feelings seem to be almost hotwired. Mastering some amount of control over emotions is an essential skill, one your youth will apply again and again throughout life. Being able to diffuse their anger or hurts, express themselves with honesty and integrity, and tap into empathy all equate to healthy self-development and relationships. In short, youth learn to work and play well with others. But learning to "self-master" emotional reactions to people and events takes youth a step further: Self-mastery is one of the essential elements of living from a strength-based approach, of harnessing one's own power.

As important as the art of managing emotions is, it is seldom taught until one gets into a "red alert" situation, such as having to attend an anger management class or entering into therapy as a result of behavior issues or a crisis. In this chapter you'll learn strategies for coaching young people to identify their negative feelings, resolve them, and then move on. Your youth will understand that letting go is part of being able to walk fully in their personal power, secure and confident in themselves. And, in case you're feeling a bit insecure about your own emotional development, we'll give you some solid strategies for harnessing your emotions when conflict is on the verge of erupting in your group.

Emotions and Youth

We are all born with a range of strong emotions. Some of our emotions can cause us to see red, have a cry fest, or erupt into deep belly laughs. Emotions can motivate us to take action in the cause of justice or in the heat of the moment. Emotions are part of what make us so very human, and they color our expressions of ourselves, our views on the world, and our opinions of other people.

For young people especially, emotions can feel overwhelming. Growing up is not easy, in part because youth is a time of feeling everything! We know that, developmentally, young people's brains are maturing and hormones are active. Young people are still in the beginning stages of learning how to identify their emotions, work through them, and manage them. Their emotions can be raw, resulting in a lot of drama. As your group journeys together, you will experience some trying moments. These moments tend to happen when someone is frazzled or hasn't eaten enough or gotten enough sleep. Or, sometimes the diverse personalities, needs, and wants of a group start to collide and emotions run high. As a youth leader, you will sometimes be in the position of trying to master the emotions of your group to avoid unnecessary conflicts.

We will provide you with some solid strategies for running a group when emotions run high, but first, let's talk about emotional intelligence.

Emotional Intelligence

When we help young people identify and know what they feel, understand *why* they feel what they do, and channel those feelings—use them—in positive ways, then we're helping them build their emotional intelligence. Emotional intelligence covers everything from self-awareness to relationship management. Building its capacity can affect how you behave. You are more aware of how your emotions impact your thoughts, and with practice you can control knee-jerk responses, change your own thoughts, and adapt to what's going on. A high emotional intelligence also impacts how you interact with others. You're more likely to pick up on emotional cues, communicate clearly, and empathize.

STRATEGIC

MOVES

- *Identifying emotions is good for self-awareness and for learning to read others. Use an emotional expressions chart (see webpage link listed on page 219) for "emotional check-ins." Let each person point out which facial expression he or she most identifies with today.*
- *Have youth sit in a circle and think of a weather pattern that describes their emotional barometer today ("partly cloudy," "sunny and bright," or "dangerous storm ahead").*
- *Write down various emotions on cards and have participants act out what that emotion looks like using both face and body language.*

Where's the Stress? . . . .

One of the benefits of having emotional intelligence is that it can help you manage your emotions in positive ways to relieve stress, face and overcome challenges, and even defuse conflict. Try to identify different parts of the body where people tend to feel or hold emotions when they are stressed. This might include the nape of the neck, between the shoulder blades, or in the pit of your stomach. Start with a relaxation technique to illustrate how your body feels when tense versus relaxed: have everyone tense their feet, hold for a count of five, let go, pause for a few breaths to allow time to pass and silence to enter, tense their calves, hold, let go, pause, and then continue up the body. This exercise stimulates body awareness and emotional awareness.

Leader's tip: Creating a safe environment is critical to the success of this activity. Let your youth know that this should be a quiet reflective time to be in one's own personal space. Admit that it might feel a little awkward or unusual, but challenge them to try this new way of being peaceful and reflective.

. . . .

Reading Emotions in Others

It's important to help youth become aware of not only their emotions but also how others may be feeling. Becoming part of a community requires that youth move from a "me-centered" space to a "we-centered" space. To help develop that aspect of emotional intelligence, you need to help youth develop empathy, that ability to recognize the emotional cues of others, how they feel, and to respond in a compassionate way. With an understanding of emotions and their cues, youth will be able to better interact and engage with others. In fact, others may very well be drawn to youth who express and show sincere concern for them.

PLAYFUL MOVES

May I See Your Emotional ID?: For this game, write down several different emotions (angry, happy, sad, afraid, etc.) on sticky notes. Tape one emotion to the back of each person. If your group is large, select a handful of people to "carry" the emotions. Then have one person stand with his or her back toward the group so everyone can read the emotion on the sticky note. Then have the person turn toward the group to watch as they act out the emotion. Afterward, the person with the sticky note tries to guess what emotion is taped on his or her back.

After the game is over, talk about it. Ask them questions: How did you feel when everyone acted a certain way toward you? How did it feel to have lots of angry looks, sad looks, or happy faces directed at you? How do our emotions impact others? What can we do to deal with our emotions in healthy ways?

Teaching Self-Mastery to Your Youth

Our ongoing theme throughout this book has been one of strength and personal power. What we hope you understand about emotions and power is this: If we can help youth understand, harness, and self-manage their emotions, if we can develop that capacity and self-power, the outcome will show in how they act. As they learn to exert power and gain self-mastery, the behaviors that cause us concern will naturally change.

Helping youth self-master their emotions begins with helping them identify feelings and label how they are feeling. The second step is to teach them how to self-manage emotions—whether disruptive or positive—so that they can be their true selves. You can accomplish the latter by consistently using these three strategies: maintaining norms, guiding them toward positive actions, and leveraging positive peer pressure.

Maintain the Norm . . . Daily

Early on, we talked about the importance of establishing norms. Norms, when maintained, help youth to feel emotionally safe, and they provide guidance for consequences of behaviors, which are often the result of out-of-control, runaway emotions. Use those norms. Guide, invite, and encourage your group to take action toward positive group dynamics. And keep the goal in mind: teaching them to control themselves. Maintaining norms as a daily practice can help you put into place the expectation of self-mastery and responsibility.

When a group breaks from meeting for any length of time—for spring, fall, or a holiday break—remember that your youth are away from the group's routine and habits. Whenever you reconvene as a group after any length of time away from each other, revisit the norms and reestablish a calm, consistent environment and routine.

Guide and Invite Young People toward the Positive

Emotions are strong and can color decision-making abilities and behavior choices unless youth learn to manage their emotions. Redirecting their emotions and energies toward positive outlets helps them learn to take control of impulse feelings and behaviors, self-manage, and deliberately choose the direction they want to go. As a leader focused on identifying and building strengths, always look to "catch 'em doing good." Point out what your youth are doing right. Help them become aware of when they contribute in good ways to the overall group. Give ongoing positive feedback. Accentuate the positives and redirect the negatives before they get out of hand. Consistently uphold behavioral expectations and don't tire of doing so. You don't know what the other adults in your young people's lives are doing. You may be the one constant person who creates a positive, stable environment and consistently upholds behavioral expectations. You may be the difference.

Allison Hurst, a youth worker, shares how she challenged a student to use his leadership power as a positive force, rather than a disruptive one, both to impact the emotional climate of the group and to challenge him to take control of his choices:

> I had a student who always led the others in negative behaviors and disrespect. I pulled him aside and told him that whether he wanted the responsibility or not, he was the clear leader of the group. I then said that because everyone was acting disrespectfully, my doing crowd control was prohibiting us from doing anything fun or accomplishing any goals. I suggested we work out a deal. I said that if he would help me out by leading students into respecting me and participating, then I would make sure to plan really fun and engaging activities that I knew everyone would enjoy. He stared at me and asked, "Do you really think I'm that much of a leader?"
>
> I looked at him and said, "Without a doubt. Try me. I dare you."
>
> He held out his hand and told me I had a deal. When we went back into the classroom, all it took was for him to pay attention and then say something along the lines of "Y'all she's talking. Let's see what she's got," and all of a sudden everyone was on board. The two of us shared a secret grin and the rest of the summer was mostly smooth sailing. It's amazing what a leadership role can do for a student's attitude and behavior. If we give them the chance, they will rise to the occasion.

Allison's story illustrates the power of inviting youth to do good and leverage their power and, in this case, that included emotional power. Allison challenged the young man to step it up, get his behavior and emotions under control, and move beyond his own interests to leading and thinking about the group. Youth want power. You can show them how to use it responsibly and as a force for the common good.

Leverage Positive Peer Pressure

Leveraging positive peer pressure helps engage those who are further along in their emotional intelligence, or those who aren't struggling at the moment with their emotions, to offer support, encouragement, and help in making good choices. When disruptions occur, look for opportunities to invite youth to step into power. Involve them as coconspirators in self-managing the emotions of the group. For example, if someone starts to dominate the group in a negative way, encourage individuals to step up and take leadership. If someone starts taking over the group and doing all the talking, look around and observe faces. Recall the goals they've set. Look for someone you can tell has something to say but hasn't been able to. Or look for someone who has said, "I want to learn to speak up more in the group." You might interject, "Jose, how are feeling right now?" instead of asking Darcy to quit talking. This creates an opportunity for Jose to speak up and redirect the group.

In both of these situations, you are quietly inviting the group to self-monitor, asking the group how they can collaborate and cooperate together to change the situation. A wise adult will shift from being directive to leveraging positive power in the group to continue to expand power. It's important to let youth practice the art of self-control, decision making, and courage, which are all part of that emotional puzzle that each person must learn to solve.

If it is a one-on-one situation, remember to resist the urge to "fix it" for them. Instead, help young people realize the emotions involved, and help them find a solution that will bring the situation back to balance. For example, when a young person comes up with a complaint about a peer, defer back to that young person. Help him or her think about what to do and determine a course of action. Help youth find their power. Ask, "What do you think we should do about it?"

If adults constantly manage the emotions of young people, they will never learn to do it themselves. We must help them find safe places to navigate their feelings and iron them out safely and wisely. Ask questions and guide the group, but don't automatically be the expert, the arbitrator, or the problem solver. Conflict and managing emotions are events that will happen throughout their lifetimes, so youth must start practicing at a young age. The more they get to practice handling emotions and learning to deal with them well, the better off they will be.

Always guide and invite. While never letting the group get out of control, encourage them toward positive group dynamics where all are valued. As you encourage them toward creating that safe, welcoming group, they will start to step up to help create the space.

100 Questions

100 Questions: Keep an envelope of questions on hand. When you are having difficulty getting a young person to talk about what's bothering him or her, use a conversation starter to get the ball rolling. Have him or her pull out a question for you to answer. Next, you pull out a different question for him or her to answer. Keep going back and forth. Once your youth is relaxed, check in to see if he or she wants to talk about what is going on or if he or she is ready to go back to the group.

Tips for Helping Youth Harness Their Emotional Power

Keep in mind these tips that Elizabeth Parrot, a school counselor, recommends to help young people harness their power:

Let kids fail. Don't fix everything for them. People learn from mistakes and that's where confidence comes from. If we fix everything, youth won't learn how to live in the tough moments. As they learn to manage their emotions, they are sure to make big blunders. They will blurt out feelings in an inappropriate context, tempers will explode in public places, and they will say hurtful things. After the mistakes happen, talk through the circumstances, and help young people identify ways that they can reconcile any hurt relationships and plan new behavior patterns for future situations.

Sometimes those unfortunate moments happen with other adults and have long-lasting effects. Once a young person was acting silly and told his teacher off. Afterward, he said he felt powerful saying what he did. He didn't understand at the time that consequences are connected to using one's power. In his failure to harness his power and control his emotions, in his mistaken idea of acting on power, he ultimately disempowered himself. He created a situation in which the teacher he yelled at was going to remember what he did and that memory would more than likely impact how she treated him in the future. He learned a valuable lesson about understanding emotional power and the importance of using it responsibly. He figured out quickly that he needed to learn self-mastery.

Recognize that their brains and their bodies may be developing faster than they want. Youth often feel like everyone's watching them; they feel like they have their own audience watching and waiting to see how they will do, waiting for them to make a mistake, for them to fail. Empathize with young people. Use gentle humor to lighten situations. The world is not ending because something embarrassing happens. Help them learn to laugh at themselves and realize that everyone makes mistakes. Help them learn not to take themselves so seriously.

Listen. Are you listening with eyes, ears, and heart? Or are you listening with what you will say next? Listening is the most important thing. Young people don't want you to fix them. They just want their voices to be heard. When they feel supported, they will have more courage to look at their behaviors and consider changes that need to be made.

STRATEGIC

MOVES

Elizabeth Parrot suggests the following ideas.

- *When youth come to you with an issue they are having a hard time talking about, ask them to write about it. Once they write it all out, you'll be able to separate the issues and tackle them individually.*
- *Keep art supplies and paper on hand. If youth need a moment to deal with emotions, let them write or draw to untangle their feelings.*
- *Have your youth create a playlist to listen to when they need a moment to collect themselves. Give them the space to feel successful and the confidence to self-regulate.*

Your Emotional Boundaries

As adults, we, too, benefit from being able to identify our feelings. Obviously, we can't share all of our feelings with the young people we work with. Our focus when we are with them is *on* them. It's not that we can't share the fact that we're sad or having a bad day. Our emotions and thoughts are somewhat like an onion—with many layers. Everyone in our programs will see the outer layers. They know if we're having a bad day. Young people we work with consistently will start to see the next layer of our thoughts and feelings. However, what we share—if anything—should only be revealed if it helps create a teachable moment for them. We have our own adult friends to help us deal with our problems. We are the role models and we need to maintain solid boundaries that reflect our roles as coaches and guides.

De-escalating Conflict

Plato said, "Be kind, for everyone you meet is fighting a hard battle." That's good insight to keep in mind as you strive to do things from a strength-based approach, especially in the challenging times, or those "zooey" moments in your group.

No group is perfect. No matter what the age of your youth, tempers can flare. People get hot, tired, irritable, cranky. During these times, whatever they have learned about handling emotions may go out the window and conflict happens. At this point, the question becomes, How will you handle it? Following are a few points to keep in mind during heated moments in your group.

Be kind but firm. Try to nip things in the bud before they escalate. Use your sense of humor to deflate situations or to bring an individual back in line. Give an example of an "out": "You didn't really mean to call him a chowderhead, did you? You meant to call him Brad, right?" Help them to backpedal, fast! At the same time, model correct responses and behaviors.

Draw from the strength of your relationship with your youth. Your first tactic in building your group was to build relationships, right? It's much easier to address conflicts if you have a working relationship. A strong working relationship gives you a solid base from which to operate. You've established an amount of trust and safety. You have already been looking for the good within each youth, and during conflict, it's the perfect time to tap into those qualities to diffuse the situation.

Offer perspective. Sometimes conflict can be easily abated if and when youth understand that people are looking at things from different perspectives or simply have different opinions. Those situations are great for teaching the importance of listening, seeking to understand each other, and applying critical thinking skills. For example, if a group gets hot over opinions on "who has it harder: boys or girls?," then you have an ideal opportunity to talk about different experiences and opinions, and to remind them that they wouldn't argue over which favorite color is the best. They would accept that as just an opinion shaped by experiences, exposure, and preferences. Why not adopt the same attitude over other issues?

What Do You Do with Conflict? . . . .

Circle the number that best reflects your response to the following statements, with 1 being not so good and 5 being incredibly good:

I handle conflicts in a caring, respectful manner—
  privately and humbly. 1 2 3 4 5

I admit to my mistakes or bad decisions and teach
  youth to do the same. 1 2 3 4 5

I admit when I don't know something. 1 2 3 4 5

I share hopes and dreams, and talk about what it takes
  to achieve them. 1 2 3 4 5

Be yourself. Don't cave in to the pressure to be perfect all the time or feel as if you have to keep up the front of having all of life together. Be willing to make mistakes and be vulnerable—for yourself but also for their sakes. That's the key. It has to be for them, not you. Trust them with your mistakes and get vulnerable with them so they will know that trust is a two-way street in your relationship.

When Conflict Is a Power Struggle

In conflict, the real issue is that there are two or more differing opinions trying to live in the same space. How can differing opinions share the same space without causing damage to either party? How can opinions be shared and respected without deteriorating into a struggle for power that looks like "I'm right; you're wrong"?

Many conflicts boil down to power struggles. When our immediate reaction is to judge, fix, or attempt to save someone, we are trying to usurp power. All of these responses assume that we know more, can fix the situation somehow, or can save the person in question if he or she would just take our advice. When we assume these things, each response sets us up to be more powerful than the other person. The result is that it shuts down conversation, and we are no longer listening. Countering that urge to struggle calls for a higher level of thinking—a hard thing to remember at any age!

Conversation versus Debate

A higher level of thinking requires that we stop concerning ourselves with who is right and who is wrong. That's debatable anyway, and in truth it's beside the point. The real point is to engage in a conversation, not an argument. A higher level of thinking allows us to exchange ideas and deepen friendships, and steers us away from power struggles based on coming out ahead and being right.

If you can teach your youth to hear each other out with respect and to listen for deeper stories, they will come to have a deeper understanding of each other. Relationships will flourish. Understanding will blossom. It all has to do with power and how youth use that power.

The next time conflict happens in your group, teach your youth to ask themselves, *What's the higher good in our relationship? Do I value our relationship more than the issue that we don't see eye to eye on? If so, can I give up the need to be right and curb my need to judge, fix, or save? Can I listen?*

Diversity Toss from *Great Group Games:* You will need two beach balls. Label one "F" (for first and fun) and write lighthearted, easy-to-answer questions on them, such as "What's your favorite color?" Label the other beach ball "S" (for second and serious) and write more difficult-to-answer questions on them, such as "Who has it harder—boys or girls?" Have players toss the "F" ball gently from one person to another. Whoever catches the ball reads aloud the question nearest their right thumb and answers it. Pass the ball until everyone's had a turn. Players have the right to pass if they don't like a question, or they can choose to answer a different question. After everyone has had a turn, collect the "F" ball and toss out the "S" ball. Repeat the game using the new ball until all have had a turn. Remind players to respect each other's opinions. Discuss the differences between the two balls:

- How hard was it to answer the questions on the first ball? The second?

- How many of you wanted to say something when someone else was expressing his or her opinions?

- How well do you listen to others when people are talking about something that is important to you? How can you listen more effectively to others?

- How can learning to listen help minimize conflicts?

- What can you do to encourage peaceful conflict resolution?

How People Respond to Conflict

How people respond to conflict depends on a lot of different factors. Common responses are often based on emotions. We know the brain has a fight-or-flight mode. If that mode is activated by stress, then most people are naturally wired to respond by either attacking conflict (fight mode) or running from conflict (flight mode). Neither of these options is necessarily healthy (unless you are being physically threatened and then, by all means, getting away to a safe place is prudent), so it's important to talk with youth about recognizing their tendencies and learning to respond to conflict in a healthy way.

Beyond fight or flight, we all have a "trained" response to conflict, one we learned growing up. We may be passive, passive-aggressive, aggressive, or assertive. In general, passive responders allow others to have complete control and power of the situation. They give up their power and often don't even recognize they have power in the first place. A passive-aggressive person acts as if they don't care or are giving up power, but secretly they are furious. They take out their aggression indirectly, by gossiping or trying to make someone feel guilty. People may never really know how the passive-aggressive person feels about a given situation. Others respond with pure aggression, attacking with words or actions when they feel threatened. They lash out at and try to hold at bay the person who, or the situation that, is making them feel uncomfortable.

Luckily, these aren't our only options. As we learn self-mastery over our emotions, breathe deeply, and think, we can put our emotional intelligence to work on our behalf. We can own our feelings and take appropriate action. This response is an assertive response. Assertive responders are honest, thoughtful, and firm in their responses. Instead of accusing or blaming others, they share feelings by using statements such as, "When _____ happens, I feel _____." They name their feelings, acknowledge the feelings of others involved, and seek to find a resolution.

Ask young people to consider their natural responses to conflict, and ask each person to consider how he or she might respond in a healthier way during future conflicts. Once you get into this conversation, more than likely you'll be asked for ideas on how to deal with conflict in better ways. The skill of meeting and overcoming conflicts isn't inbred. It's a learned skill. Within this section of the book, we want to note that part of dealing with conflict comes from self-mastery of emotions. Self-mastery of emotions can be mightily influenced by the simple act of learning to regulate one's breath, getting still, focusing on the present moment, and recognizing that within you all is just as it should be—a calm pool of stillness is there that is your natural state of being.

Teach youth about the power of silence. The practice of quiet time can slow things down into a rhythm. Trying to "be present" and focus on what's going on in this moment can help counter negativity and even deescalate conflicts from red alert back to neutral. When the brain hits fight-or-flight mode, it takes a bit of work to think again and move beyond emotions. The brain, and the person, responds well to meditation, as we noted in chapter 3. But we don't want you to take our word for it. We want you to see it and hear it for yourselves from young people and adults who've integrated the practice of "quiet time" into their schools and groups. See the For Your Bookshelf section on page 219 for links to four videos that demonstrate the power of quiet to prevent violence, improve grades, and ultimately allow young people to tap inside to activate their inner power to respond from a place of stillness.

Influencing Behaviors in Conflict

As you model how to resolve conflict peacefully, consider these methods to talk through arguments when they happen.

Pull aside the one or two people in conflict to a semi-private place for the conversation. You don't want to embarrass or shame the youth by having public confrontations. Shaming and making the young person feel uncomfortable won't get you anywhere in promoting your cause for positive behavior and tends to do more harm than good.

Use a quiet, calm voice. Reprimanding with a loud voice can fuel anger, frustration, or even bitterness, whereas using a quiet voice helps create a calm environment for you and the youth.

If moderating between two youth, ask them to sit face-to-face and look each other in the eye. Ask them to talk directly to each other and calmly explain their frustrations. (Don't tattle to the adult but talk to each other.)

Encourage them to be quick to say, "I'm sorry" for a wrong, assumed or real. If they don't think they've done something wrong, but the other person is convinced that an offense has been committed, encourage "offenders" to recognize and validate the "victim's" feelings. For example, "Nathan, I'm sorry if you think I hit you on purpose. I didn't mean to, and I'll try to watch where I'm walking in the future so I don't bump into you."

Remind parties to assume the best about the other person. Rarely is someone "out to get you." Conflicts often happen from misunderstandings and conversations can often set things right.

Once the conflict has been discussed, agree to move forward and move on. Let the conflict go and refuse to take it into the future. It's done.

Learning how to handle conflict is tricky! It is not an instinct instilled at birth. Conflict resolution is a learned skill that needs to be practiced many times before it becomes second nature. Offer grace to your youth and let them know they can do it and that the skills they are learning will be valuable throughout their lives. Be patient. Keep in mind that in each situation, your purpose is to put the young person first and the results last. As you make it about them, the result you want to see will come.

STRATEGIC

MOVES

- *Peer mediation is a viable response when two or more are in conflict and can't find resolutions themselves. Look to see if there are peer mediators in your group or at your school, or consider training interested members in your group.*
- *Use a conflict-style survey with your group to help youth identify their natural response to conflict and what steps they personally need to work on to deal with conflict well.*

- *If and when you need to have tough or vulnerable conversations, find a quiet and private place to talk. Protect your young person's vulnerability as much as possible and make sure he or she knows that there is nothing more important to you at this moment than having the conversation.*
- *Assure youth that you will keep your conversations confidential unless it involves harm to themselves or another person.*

Dealing with Conflict One-on-One

The book *Building Developmental Assets in School Communities* offers tips for dealing one-on-one with the instigator of conflict to help influence behaviors in a positive way. We adapted and expanded a few of their ideas included below:

Use their name. This communicates respect and attention.

Identify the inappropriate behavior. Stick with facts in this reflection—no shaming or expressing your own feelings. Don't, for instance, say you were disappointed or worried, which only tends to add to the negativity.

Indicate that the behavior does not match up with how you see them. Emphasize the good and the potential that you know is within them. In *The Dark Knight Rises,* there's a scene where Batman asks Catwoman, a burglar, to help people in the city escape. She responds by asking why she should help or get involved and declares that she's not that good of a person. He responds by saying that she is stronger than that. He lets her know that he sees something valuable within her (even though she doesn't see it in herself). In the end, she lives up to what he believes about her. Look for the good within. Mirror it to the young person.

Ask them what happened. Indicate that you understand but that what they did was inappropriate. Give them the opportunity to share and think through their actions. Reiterate what is wrong and why.

Model a different way. Ask them to show you an appropriate way to respond, a better way to handle the situation. If they get stuck, ask them if they want you to model a response.

Encourage them. Always close tough conversations with a word of encouragement and thanks. Thank them for listening and express your belief in them to do things differently and better next time: "I believe in you." "I know you can be the person you want to be." "I've seen you make progress in this area, and I know you're going to grow more and more." "I care for you, and I will walk with you as you struggle with this issue. Know that you won't be working on this alone."

EXERCISE

✎ When Emotions Are High . . . .

How do you respond when emotions in your group are running high? Place a check mark by the actions you usually take. Highlight actions you would like to try.

☐ I don't jump to conclusions about youth involved in conflict because of their pasts. I look at each situation based on its own merit.

☐ I acknowledge everyone's feelings during conflict.

☐ I help them acknowledge their feelings and own their actions.

☐ I speak calmly. I resist the urge to respond in anger or aggression myself.

☐ I stop myself from cutting people off or interrupting them when they're explaining what happened to cause the conflict.

☐ I look for strengths at play during conflict resolution so that I can try to empower youth with their own resources.

☐ I defer power to youth. I ask them what they think they should do to resolve the conflict. I try to encourage them to initiate solutions themselves.

☐ I follow up after conflicts to see how they are doing and check to see whether they're following through with their game plans.

☐ I listen to both sides and don't play favorites. I seek to make the space safe for all parties.

Based on this quick assessment, are there adjustments you need to make regarding the way you help young people handle conflicts?

- -

Dealing with Complex Challenges beyond Our Know-How

Sometimes the challenges we have in our group come from outside forces we may never learn about. These forces could be related to mental, physical, or emotional well-being or caused by situations in the home or neighborhood. Sometimes helping youth learn to harness power and be safe means involving other loving adults and professionals. None of us is automatically equipped to deal with every problem that comes along with our children.

Lean On Your Network

No matter how great the challenge, you are not alone. When you are concerned about a young person's well-being, talk with the parents. If you're not sure whether it's appropriate to involve the parents, by all means, check with your agency or school guidelines. If you need advice, ask a trusted mentor. If you do talk to parents, have the courage to speak with them in a humble and loving way. Whether the parents are seeing the same concerns, or you are the one to open their eyes, the circle of support for that young person will immediately expand. Youth may view their parents as the enemy, but many parents are their child's strongest ally. Parents deserve the chance to act in the best interest of their child. That can't happen unless they are informed.

Beyond parents, there are others who can help when tough calls need to be made. You have your supervisor, trained professionals (social workers, counselors, psychologists, clergy, teachers), and even the police. Trained professionals will provide support and education to help you do the best you can to ensure your youths' safety and well-being.

Always follow your agency and state policies regarding the reporting of sexual and physical abuse. As mandatory reporters, youth workers and teachers have a legal obligation to report suspected cases of abuse.

Educate Yourself

Internet search engines make it easy to find the information and resources you need. Use it to educate yourself on what you want to learn. For example, searches on common issues resulted in these reliable sources:

- National Institute on Alcohol Abuse and Alcoholism, www.niaaa.nih.gov/.
- Anxiety and Depression Association of America, www.adaa.org/.
- Children and Adults with Attention-Deficit/Hyperactivity Disorder, www.chadd.org.
- National Child Abuse Hotline, 1-800-4-A-CHILD (1-800-422-4453), www.childhelp.org.
- Cyberbullying Research Center, http://www.cyberbullying.us/.
- National Eating Disorders Association, www.nationaleatingdisorders.org.
- National Alliance on Mental Health, www.nami.org.
- National Suicide Prevention Lifeline, www.suicidepreventionlifeline.org.

Look at the Heart

As you face tough challenges or unexpected hurdles that throw you for a loop, remember kids are just kids. No matter what the issue or difficulty, they don't want to be treated or seen as different. A child with a mental illness is just a child. A child with a physical challenge is just a child. A child with a learning difference is just a child. They have special needs (we all do!), but they just want to be seen as normal people. Keep them in mind first: see them, not the issues they are struggling with. Don't let a person be defined by their circumstances or their challenges. Look past the exterior casing to focus on the heart, the core of who each person really is.

When to Involve a Professional

If and when a time comes when a youth tells you that someone is thinking about or planning to hurt himself or herself, or hurt someone else, we want you to remember three things:

1. Your youth are listening very closely to you and watching how you will react to them. Give them that credit and don't underestimate them. As they share, be a mirror of support. "Even when the information they give you is shocking or painful to hear," says case manager Joan Embree, "you can't relay that response to them. It could increase their pain or shame. You have to be the face of love and acceptance." You have to be nonjudgmental. Whatever the struggle, it's important that you create a safe space for them in which you listen and engage. And love. And accept.

2. Their trust may be fragile, but that can't stop you from seeking support. Ask them to trust you to connect them to someone who will be able to help them further (another agency, counselor, police officer, or pastor). They've come to you; now you need to help them take the next step to gain further help and power to make things right. Remind them that you have

their best interests at heart. Remind them of your support. And then get the help they need. If you are not a trained counselor, you must expand your team and involve an expert. It's the right thing to do. You can't do it all. And they need the expertise that trained professionals offer.

3. When those calls need to be made, use your best judgment to both protect your youth and empower them. Consider the best way to involve your youth in the process; it might take all their strength just to tell you about the difficult situation, leaving them totally depleted. Or, they may need to take that next step with you. If you have to call the Department of Children's Services, for example, you might want to have the young person there with you, if he or she would like to be there. Involve youth as far as you can in the process so that they are in the know and can maintain personal power. But only involve youth if it contributes to their overall well-being. Assess the situation and the youth involved, listen to your gut, and always treat each young person with kindness and respect.

Keepers. . . . .

What do you want to remember from this chapter? What might you use or try? Flip back through the chapter and skim for possibilities or keepers. Record the ideas that intrigue you, seem possible, or make you excited.

FOR YOUR BOOKSHELF

"Emotions Vocabulary Chart," Anger Management Institute of Texas, www.ami-tx.com/Portals/3/EmotionsFlyer.pdf.

School Fights End at Detroit School Thanks to Meditation, YouTube, www.youtube.com/watch?v=fbgCK8pUED8.

Violence Rate Down 50% and Grades Up with Meditation in AZ School, YouTube, www.youtube.com/watch?v=GUZRIX_SlHU.

Violence in School Ends Thanks to David Lynch and Meditation, YouTube, www.youtube.com/watch?v=93-NzNBLCbE.

Quiet Time Program in San Francisco Schools, YouTube, www.youtube.com/watch?v=fz-rB6aKnSU.

Training Peer Helpers: Coaching Youth to Communicate, Solve Problems, and Make Decisions (second edition), by Barbara B. Varenhorst (Search Institute Press, 2011).

. . . .

The Practice of Gratitude

Chapter 13

We can only be said to be alive in those moments when our hearts
are conscious of our treasures.

—Thornton Wilder, playwright and novelist

What's the point of helping youth discover their inner beauty, meaning,
and giftedness if we don't teach them to take time to delight in who they
are? That's part of gratitude. Gratitude is simply the act of being grateful.
Being grateful that I am strong and healthy, even if I didn't score any points
in the basketball game. Being grateful for the way my brain works, even if I
performed poorly on the SAT. Being grateful for my friend who really ap-
preciates me, even when I was shunned by the popular group. Being grateful
for the opportunity to work with this group of young people, even if it challenges me to my very core. A strength-based approach depends on focusing
on what's right about people—and that naturally extends to you and the
people in your personal life. We need to remind ourselves and our young
people to be grateful, so this chapter will explore ideas to help you and your
youth practice an attitude of gratitude.

The Benefits of Gratitude

Gratitude changes attitudes, as it helps people focus on the good, instead of
dwelling on the negative. This is powerful, because a person's attitude pro-
foundly impacts his or her life. Gratitude is a power practice that changes
our perspectives about life's joys and hardships. It recharges our batteries

when our energy is depleted or we are overwhelmed by life. Having a grateful spirit can reduce stress and lead to better overall health. Gratitude revitalizes and rejuvenates us.

The discipline of gratitude can help you attract more of the positives in life and experience greater satisfaction because good things naturally follow people who bring out the best in others. Learning to see, acknowledge, sustain, and express gratitude is a strength-based practice and discipline worth the effort.

Disciplines to Foster Gratitude

Some personalities have a tendency to be more negative than positive. Just as gratitude and a positive, happy heart can beget good energy, negativity in an individual or group can have a powerful and lasting influence. We know that it takes 21 days to create a new habit. Some of us might take that long or longer to start seeing the positive; fortunately, the more positive we put out there, the more we will get in return. Here are some tips to help you establish the habit of gratitude.

Decide. Decide you're going to be as present as you can to each moment and find the joy. Many times we are surrounded by joys we don't see because we're too focused on the next deadline or project. Decide to live in the present moment and fully experience it.

Every day, embrace what's good. When something good happens, don't cut it off in your hurry to move on! Stop, note it, recognize it, and receive it as the gift it is.

Hit replay. Savor what's good. Re-picture it and turn it into an experience. Feel those feelings again; feel them in your body—the peace, the sense of wonder. Stay with those good feelings and memories for as long as you can. Why not? Prolonging the experience can deepen and magnify the memory. Reliving good things is worth it. Besides, it takes repetition for the brain to make experiences into long-term memories. Store up those good moments!

Share gratitude. The act of sharing is a happiness booster. And it brings its own reason to be grateful. Giving of ourselves is a quick way to access gratitude. Can you hold open a door? Help someone cross the street? Change a lightbulb? Take a moment to listen? Share an encouraging word? Give a hug or a smile? In giving, you find much to be grateful for. That's a double gratitude!

STRATEGIC

MOVES

- *Have youth create a list of the little blessings, joys, and graces that they have experienced recently. Encourage them to use words, phrases, or even pictures.*
- *Allow youth time to journal about things they are grateful for each day. Ask them to be attentive to the changes they see in their attitude as they journal.*
- *Include a "circle of gratitude" time, inviting each person to share one thing he or she is grateful for; pause after each person shares.*
- *Ask youth to choose a joyful event or moment they experienced and relive it in as much detail as they can in their journal. Provide colored pencils if they want to draw the experience. As they linger over the memory and savor it, they begin to root it more deeply into memory, putting deposits into their gratitude bank.*

TAKE TWO Take a couple of moments to ponder these questions:

How might my attitude change the spirit of my group today?
Or even one young person's perspective?

How could my attitude change my own spirit today?

What I Am Grateful For . . . .

Use the letters from the word *gratitude* to help young people think about people or things they appreciate as they create an acrostic. Here are some examples:

G: *G*reg smiled the biggest smile today. I love his smile.

R: *R*eceived a thank-you note from a friend for helping him through a rough patch.

G

R

A

T

I

T

U

D

E

Smile Power . . . .

Read together: *"A smile costs nothing but gives much. It enriches those who receive without making poorer those who give. It takes but a moment, but the memory of it sometimes lasts forever. None is so rich or mighty that he cannot get along without it, and none is so poor that he cannot be made rich by it. Yet a smile cannot be bought, begged, borrowed, or stolen, for it is something that is of no value to anyone until it is given away. Some people are too tired to give you a smile. Give them one of yours, as none needs a smile so much as he who has no more to give."*—Unknown

Talk to your youth about the ramifications of positive and negative attitudes. Ask them about the power of attitudes to change a situation for good or worse. Challenge the group to share their smiles widely and freely even when they don't feel like it! Their smiles might make the difference. Think about other ways they can reinforce positive attitudes. What can they do?

. . . .

Having a Happy Heart

Grateful people are usually happy people. Everything is probably not going their way in life, but they are choosing to focus on the good energy around them. They realize that life's challenges don't last forever; what happens to them or around them doesn't have to define who they are or how they respond to what is going on. They choose to live with a happy heart. And they know that the very choice to focus on the good magnifies the good because what we focus on with our attention increases. It's the law of attraction.

Having a happy heart doesn't happen naturally for everyone. Ironically, it takes work to "be" happy, to choose happy. When focusing on developing a happy heart in yourself or in your group, consider these daily disciplines.

For every negative thing you say, state two positives to negate the bad juju and reinstate positive vibes. This tactic comes from counselor Elizabeth Parrot.

Use visual cues to remind yourself to be grateful. Post a favorite quote someplace where you will see it every day. Or put a string on your finger or wear a bracelet on your arm to remind you to focus on good things. Every time you catch yourself saying something negative, move the bracelet to your other arm as a reminder to start again. Forgetfulness is often the force that blocks us from being grateful, so create a visual reminder.

Use an inspirational daily reading or look at things that make you happy. Some examples are the comics, a favorite blog, stories of kindness, the sunset, or photos on Pinterest.

First thing in the morning, before rushing headlong into the day, jump into gratitude and say out loud or in your head three or four things that make you happy. Name little things, maybe even the ones that you take for granted, such as hot showers, coffee, the coveted best seat at the coffee shop, or the fact that all your toes wiggle just as they should.

Always note the smallest efforts and successes. As you start your day, you can probably bank on the fact that not everything will go perfectly. So, why not start the day by identifying five things you have control over. Examples include brushing your teeth, telling your children you love them as they go off to school, getting in a 10-minute workout before breakfast, or saying no to that extra donut. We aren't perfect. Our days aren't perfect. But there are gifts in each day and we have a choice: we can look for things to be thankful for, or we can disregard positive things that happened because they didn't quite meet our expectations. If you choose to be thankful and magnify that thanks by acknowledgment, you create more of the very energy you want in your life.

Use the words *happy heart* and *happy day* in your daily conversations to generate happiness and remind yourself and others to think about being happy. We often end phone calls and e-mails with "happy day."

And one of our friends uses "happiness" as her password to serve as a daily reminder.

Refer to your journal for inspiration. If you keep a journal of improvements, growth, observations, and unexpected surprises, refer back to it on the hard days when you need a pick-me-up.

Look for successes around you in your youth, colleagues, and even yourself. Be quick to tell your colleagues about little victories; they most likely need encouragement too.

STRATEGIC

MOVES

- *Invite your young people to make a playlist of songs that make them happy. Play it to brighten everyone's spirits.*
- *Teach youth to carve out a happy place in their minds by visualizing a place where they feel loved and enjoy being themselves.*

Expressing Gratitude by Celebrating Others

> Highly effective leaders energize others by noticing and recognizing [the efforts of others]. They thank, appreciate, recognize, and celebrate accomplishments.
>
> —Jim Clemmer, leadership author and speaker

A natural extension of gratitude is recognition. Thoughtful recognition can be a powerful motivator and sustainer for personal growth. It says to a young person, or anyone for that matter, "I notice, I care, and I'm proud of you." When considering recognition strategies, be mindful of these four principles:

- Be authentic
- Be specific
- Be unique
- Do something special

The following story illustrates perfectly all four of these principles of recognition:

Aiden was having trouble remembering to bring his homework to class. His teacher had made it clear that if he kept forgetting, his grades would start to reflect that. Mom got a call one day at work from the teacher. Mom's immediate reaction was concern. First, the teacher let Mom know that she was on speakerphone. Then he explained that he was calling her from the classroom to let her know that Aiden had brought in his homework every day this week and that he was calling her to praise his responsibility and efforts in front of his peers and her. Mom then heard the class cheering in the background. The teacher also suggested that Aiden might enjoy a reward once home. Perhaps ice cream?

The strategy of praise here was to:

- Be authentic: The teacher spoke from the heart, recognizing Aiden's success in front of his peers.
- Give specific praise: Aiden remembered to bring his homework in every day.
- Be unique in the recognition: The teacher surprised Aiden and Mom both when he called Mom on the speakerphone and when he included her in the moment of celebration.
- Celebrate/reward his hard work in a special way: The teacher created a celebration with the phone call to Mom, the cheering in the class, and the suggestion for further reward with ice cream.

Recognition and celebration are tools in a strength-based approach that should be woven throughout your program. As we look for strengths, it makes sense that we should encourage and point out those strengths as we see them to help youth become more self-aware. Recognition and celebration reinforce positive identity, well-made choices, perseverance, individual success, or skills gained. Recognition is also a tool for celebrating group efforts, learning, growth, and successes. Acknowledgments can be done in the moment or thoughtfully planned and executed during the course of the program and at the end of a program season.

Making It Personal

Make your appreciation and recognition personal by considering what your young people like and don't like, and how they do and don't want to be recognized. Everybody has natural inclinations and a unique personality that impact how they like to be recognized or appreciated. One might be in full glory when receiving an award in front of a group of people, while another will prefer privately receiving a handwritten note. To find out what kind of recognition means the most to your youth, ask them. They will likely have no problem telling you how they like to be honored or how they like to celebrate!

Know Their Love Language

Gary Chapman has written several books on what he calls the "love languages." His work suggests that each of us has our own love language, or our primary language of receiving, understanding, and expressing love. Quality time, for example, is one way that our tanks are filled. A word of encouragement is another. Understanding the love languages is a tool that can offer insight for self-understanding and knowing your youths' natural inclinations for accepting recognition and appreciation naturally. Find out your profile at www.5lovelanguages.com/profile/.

ACTIVITY

How Do You Like to Be Shown Appreciation?. . . . . .

Try this: Gather your group into the center of the room, and tell them that you will be asking a series of questions about how they like to be shown appreciation. As you give each "answer" choice, point to a different corner of the room. Youth will respond to the question by voting with their feet and walking to the part of the room that corresponds with their answer. Pay attention to and make note of their preferences so you'll know how to honor them in ways they appreciate.

- How do you like to be shown appreciation? nomination for an award, a food gift, specific verbal praise

- How do you like to be shown appreciation? a picture of yourself with other youth, a phone call, recognized at a public event

- How do you like to be shown appreciation? a piece of art, hand-made gift, a t-shirt

- How do you like to be shown appreciation? a big hug, a framed quote/inspiration, being recognized in an article

- How do you like to be shown appreciation? invited to an event (play, movie, sporting event), a gift certificate, receiving a thank-you note

* *

You can also use knowledge of your young person's sparks to show appreciation and celebrate achievements without breaking the bank. If Jacob likes puzzles, set aside time to do puzzles with him. If Miranda likes to just have the opportunity to talk to you, spend extra time together in conversation. If most of your youth like games, designate a time to play their favorite games.

Time to Celebrate!

You can be creative, thrifty, and adventurous as you celebrate the growth and success of individuals, classes, and teams. Consider these options:

Gifts

- Make a certificate that highlights their work.
- Give them candy with a note attached:

  Starbursts—you are a star student

  Kudos—we're grateful for you

  Almond Joy—you bring joy to our group!
- Surprise them with a hot chocolate or lollipop party.
- Bake a thank-you cake or cupcakes.
- Give gift certificates to their favorite stores or restaurants.
- Make CDs or iTunes playlists with songs that commemorate their achievements.
- Provide a free meal or soda.
- Handwrite a note expressing what you appreciate about them.

Thoughtfulness

- Designate a "student of the week" parking space; if you have space for a sign, write his or her name on the sign.
- Shower them with cards throughout the year: birthdays, Valentine's Day, Thanksgiving.
- Write personal notes to young people when they are absent, letting them know you missed them and look forward to seeing them soon. (Susan still remembers her mom, Betty Ragsdale, doing this in her youth group and how much it meant to the youth.)

Opportunities

- Invite your group to a sporting event, concert, or party.
- Host a coffeehouse celebration at your building with live music and coffee treats.
- Invite youth to attend in-house workshops or leadership seminars.

- Invite family members to attend your program award ceremonies.
- Arrange for discounts to local restaurants and businesses.

Public Recognition

- Hang pictures of youth and their achievements in your building.
- Nominate them for awards and scholarships; even if they aren't selected, you can announce the nomination.
- Ask for a proclamation (recognition) from the city council/mayor's office.
- Submit an article for a newspaper, professional magazine, or the local TV news.
- Give youth job titles (displays importance of roles; can use on résumés).
- Describe their work in the company newsletter or through a display.
- Brag about them on social media—Twitter, Facebook, Flikr.com, or YouTube videos (double impact because it promotes your organization as their friends see the content).
- Invite them to speak on behalf of your agency at public events.

Your Final Celebration

The end of your program, class, or sports season provides a natural time for a closing celebration. Give young people an opportunity to reflect and share

Susan's favorite celebration in high school was the Drama Club banquet, and her peers enjoyed it as well. It wasn't the food, dressing up, or the awards that they liked. It was what they got to do during dinner that was novel and fun. Each person had a stack of notepaper they could use to write down what they appreciated about each other. She explains "We passed them via 'flunkey' freshmen who ran around all night delivering them. It was our drama instructor's sense of humor: He was finally letting us 'pass notes.' We loved it!"

thoughts about their personal growth and evolving sense of purpose. Affirm youth by saying something positive about each person in terms of character, contributions, or growth. Reflect together on how your team has grown in friendship, knowledge, and skills.

As you plan your final celebration, find out what your youth prefer. As our friend Melia Arnold, a consultant, humorously says, "We might think having Barry Manilow perform is a great idea, but what if they don't even know who Barry is?" Don't forget the possibilities of letting them plan and carry out the event. Youth will come up with meaningful ways to celebrate that you won't think of—which is part of expanding their power. Tap into the resources of your creative young leaders and party planners, and let them shine as they create the experience.

Keepers. . . . .

What do you want to remember from this chapter? What might you use or try? Flip back through the chapter and skim for possibilities or keepers. Record the ideas that intrigue you, seem possible, or make you excited.

▣ FOR YOUR BOOKSHELF

Daily Good, www.dailygood.org.

The Happiness Project, www.gretchenrubin.com.

Greater Good blog, by Rick Hanson, www.greatergood.berkeley.edu/author/
    rick_hanson.

"Gratitude Quiz," Greater Good, www.greatergood.berkeley.edu/quizzes.

The Practice of Recharging

> Significance does not come from doing more. Burnout, crabbiness, lack of gratitude . . . all of these things come from doing too much. We don't change the world by taking it *all* on.
>
> —Nicole Johnson, author

We say *yes* to the hurries of the day and the unending tasks because we say *yes* to the best job in the world: working with youth. And with this amazing job in which we get to be thoroughly entertained, amused, frustrated, stretched, and gratified as we help shape and change lives, we have the ever constant temptation to keep extending as much of our energy as possible. After all, we are invested in something that counts: people. These are our "yeses."

But too often we say *no* to the very things that will recharge our energy and help us maintain power. We say *no* to quiet, solitude, gratitude, awareness, and simplicity. Thus, we often say *no* to some of the richest, deepest parts of our own strengths and lives. Rejuvenation is a simple idea, but many of us rarely take time to actually do it and build it into our lives as an active practice. And yet, the practice brings a wealth of rewards, and it rounds out our sense of oneness and completion.

This chapter's primary purpose is to suggest strategies you can use to rest and recharge your spirit and make rejuvenation an active part of your routine. As we have talked about all through this book, our goal is to interact with youth in a strength-based way. In order for us to keep it up, we have to live from a strength-based place ourselves. That center of power only comes when we take time to tend to ourselves and recharge. When you take time to slow down, young people will ultimately benefit, not only because you will have the time, energy, wisdom, and patience to love them well and continue to be an active presence in their lives, but also because you will be modeling an essential practice for how to sustain power—one they will see in action and may begin to emulate: a model of well-being.

Gut Check:
What's Your Reaction to the Idea of Recharging?

We have had the honor over the years of meeting so many good people around the country who excel at what they do. Unfortunately, they often voice the same shared struggle: burnout. Their fire dims when they fail to take the time to replenish themselves. Early in our years of working together, we heard about a survey that showed there was a higher turnover rate in youth workers than in parking lot attendants! Wow! So, how can we sustain and care for ourselves so that we can be around for the long haul—doing the jobs we love? We have to practice slowing down.

When we say "slowing down," what's your first reaction? We wouldn't be surprised if your first thought is "Sure, when I have time, I'd love to!" That's a common reaction in today's fast-paced, 24/7 society. Wistfully, people will say, "I'll take the trip I've been looking forward to or read that book when I have time to slow down." Somehow it seems that we never really take the time to slow down. There's always another project, another deadline, something else that demands our time and expertise. So we keep putting it off. We keep putting ourselves off.

The never-stop lifestyle has to change for our sake and for the sake of our youth. The discipline of slowing down to create space for silence, solitude, and the things that fuel you and sustain you isn't a luxury. It's a necessity to keep the fires of enthusiasm burning, to maintain perspective, and to keep the body, brain, emotions, and soul sane.

The Violence of Our Times

Reflect on the following quote by Trappist monk and writer Thomas Merton: "To allow ourselves to be carried away by a multitude of conflicting concerns, to surrender to too many demands, to commit to too many projects, to want to help everyone in everything is itself to succumb to the violence of our times."

What thoughts/feelings does this quote stir in you?

What are the demands clamoring for your attention?
What is carrying you away?

Why do you think you need to stop the chaos in your life?
What needs to give?

Journal Exercise

Are You on Your Way to a Quick and Easy Burnout?

Does the pace that you're keeping overwhelm you? Does life feel like it's zooming by? Do you even know what it feels like to be present with yourself? Do you know who you are outside your professional role with young people? Do you take the time to stoke your own sparks and sense of purpose?

These important questions demand answers for the sake of your very being, your powerful life that wants to be heard and respected. Our hope is that you will reflect on your needs and listen to your own wisdom as you think through these questions:

What kind of pace are you keeping? How do you react to the demands around you? Do you . . .

- Try to please everybody? Never say no?
- Carefully scrutinize everything and demand perfection?
- Think of yourself as a superhero? Do you really think that you can do everything yourself without the help of others?
- Believe that your self-worth depends on your performance?
- Skip sleep because you have too much to do?
- Try to impress others by juggling multiple projects?
- Berate yourself for failures or setbacks saying, "I should have done more?"
- Eat while you work (assuming you even take time to eat at all)?
- Fail to take days off?

Hmm . . . Did your answers catch your attention? If you said yes to four or more, see that as a red flag. It's time to make a change. Burnout is nigh! Challenge yourself to make *yourself* a priority and to take good care of you. After all, you want to continue to be motivated to serve young people for years to come. We need you. They need you. And you need you to be your best self.

. . . .

The Connection between Self-Care and Attitudes

Did you know that eating well, getting enough rest, exercising frequently, and maintaining healthy relationships and interests outside of work help you maintain a positive attitude? These are simple-sounding practices, but they are critical to maintaining well-being. Because you are impacting so many lives, your well-being is incredibly important!

Living from a Place of Centered Power

You can live in the rat race without being a rat. That's the good news! You can change the landscape of your life and have some control. It takes setting priorities, making choices, training yourself, and forming new habits. But it's worth the effort. You are worth the effort. Learning to refuel frees up energy and enthusiasm to care more for others. Seriously, if you can't take five minutes to show you care about yourself, what does that say?

Power Truths

We want to introduce you to what we call Power Truths. Power Truths are the spaces and places where we can reconnect with our own best selves and inner capacities. Power Truths are universal aids to help us find strength, wisdom, and grace for our journeys. They can help us face the most ordinary of days, make necessary decisions, and keep us grounded in being our best selves. Power Truths help us live with intention and balance, aiding us to maintain our strength and vitality.

Here we introduce Power Truths that have been particularly meaningful for our lives. Read through these Power Truths and identify what you want to adopt as habits. Your goal is to tap into your reservoir of wisdom and strength. Ultimately, you want to teach your young people how to make these disciplines their own.

Power Truth 1:
Let Go

Your well-being depends on your being able to let go of the tasks, people, or situations that are consuming your inner thoughts and attention, and that you can't control. We put this Power Truth out there first, even though it is perhaps by far the hardest to practice, because it is one you have complete power and authority to exercise. And when working with youth, you need to put this vital truth into action as quickly as you can for your own sanity.

You are good at your job because you love people well. Loving people well means you probably hear about a lot of tough issues. You probably walk with people through dark and frightening situations. You see people thrive, and you see people fail. Remember that you are not to blame for the negative choices other people make. Your job is to support, educate, encourage, and love and to be up front with young people as you see them make poor choices, humbly and lovingly questioning them about their decisions. Ultimately, they must make their own choices, and they will face the consequences. But if you worry when they make a poor choice, you are clinging to desired outcomes that are out of your control and that will eat you up on the inside. Holding on to and wasting energy on unrealistic expectations and playing events over and over again in your head take you away from what you can do.

The biggest resistance to taking time to slow down to recharge is that when you slow down, you have time to think and feel. You have to face inner turmoil that is often easier to ignore by simply staying in motion. When you slow down, there are times when your mistakes come rushing to greet and torture you. It's just life that you, too, will make mistakes and that you will miss important things. Slowing down seems like a good thing to avoid if you don't want to face the onslaught, but slowing down actually gives you the space and the power to face and let go of feelings. It invites you to acknowledge issues, accept them, learn from them, and then let them go. You don't have to beat yourself up or allow the chains of guilt to shackle you.

Guilt will impact all aspects of your well-being. Guard against this slippery slope. Letting go frees you up to recognize that it's a new day. Do your best, and know that's all you can do. When you are feeling low, discouraged, sick, or overwhelmed, let go and offer yourself grace by reminding yourself: *I do the best I can from the energy I have this day. It may not look like yesterday, or look like what I want, but I do my best from what I have today. I can be proud of today's best work.*

Finally, letting go has another very practical application. It means taking a good look at what's on your schedule. Who controls your calendar? You or outside forces that demand your attention? As you ponder what's on your calendar and what's underneath your choices, you'll find that, whether you acknowledge it or not, you are living by some creed. What does your schedule tell you? Are you living a life of deliberate intention or just passing through, tossed by whatever comes? Does your creed reflect your core beliefs, or is there a gap between your ideals and your reality? Make the decision to start letting go of the things on your calendar that don't reflect your values and priorities. And be real with yourself. Your job will never be finished—there will always be "more" to do. But you have to set a boundary somewhere. You have to say yes to taking care of yourself before you can take care of others well. Say yes to the things that are priorities and let go of the rest. A basic principle that informs how we use our time is this: *Do the thing that you were designed to do—not the things anyone can do. Use your unique skills and talents. And do the things you enjoy.* This principle helps us decide what to say no and yes to.

Balance Your Time . . . .

Jot out a basic schedule that matches your priorities for family, work, friends, and self. What do you want your weekly schedule to look like? Regularly assess the balance of your home, work, and personal lives. Some months may focus more on work, but if you know that, can you then balance the next month with other interests and needs to keep things sane?

Power Truth 2:
Be Present to the Moment

Try this for a daily discipline: *Focus on the now.* Watch how often your thoughts take you to something in the past that you can't change, to tasks on your to-do list, or to concerns about the future. Learn to pull your mind back to the present. Center your thoughts. Look around you. Notice where you are—the smells, colors, and sounds—and try to be fully present to this moment. As you rein in your thoughts to the now, observe whether you feel calmer and more at peace. Be in this moment as if no other moment were

Take the Long View

As you look back over each day, week, and year, can you honestly say you like the choices you make? Do they reflect what you say you value? For practical help, look back at the Prioritization Quiz in chapter 9.

Journal Exercise

possible. See what unfolds without trying to force anything. Don't let your worries, tasks, and thoughts control how you live. Let them go. Live in the present moment. Over time, the practice of focusing all your attention on the present moment and being in the here and now helps you slow down to a healthy pace: Your thoughts quit racing, your breathing steadies, and you feel calmer, more serene, and more connected.

STRATEGIC

MOVES

- *Take time each day to be fully aware of the sights and sounds around you. Breathe a word of thanks, capture the moment in your journal, or take a "mind picture" so you can remember the moment.*

- *Turn off the phone during meetings and time with youth, unless you are in an emergency situation. You want the person in front of you to know that he or she is the priority at that moment. Remember that people are first; technology is second.*

- *Limit the frequency of checking e-mails and voicemails. Check them at regular intervals throughout the day, instead of feeling like you must respond immediately. You are not a slave to your phone or your computer, so don't let texts, e-mails, voicemails distract you from your mission or from the person or task at hand. Give full attention to the moment.*

Power Truth 3:
Get Quiet—Befriend Stillness and Silence

In our culture, people tend to confuse the concepts of quiet and stillness and to fear the idea of "being still." Let's get the definition straight first. You can be quiet without being still by, for instance, quietly listening to others talk or quietly thinking. And you can be still without being quiet by doing something such as lying down while talking on the phone. The fear factor can creep in when you try to slow down and get both quiet and still. At that point, you've triggered an internal alarm that tries to divert you into busyness. The clamor of internal noise and buzzing thoughts is deafening! So you give up on getting quiet and still. You hang on to your "doing" and leave contemplation to the contemplatives.

Our culture encourages this "busyness." What do people often say when you ask them how they are? "I'm *so* busy." Learning to embrace silence and stillness is, then, countercultural. And, by the way, if you pitch it that way to youth, they may very well embrace those meditation practices we talked about earlier because they like being rebels and going against the current.

Silence and reflection are companions that can lead you to tap into your deep sources of wisdom and knowing. Learn to befriend silence. When you get really quiet, sit still with silence, and do not distract yourself with tasks or other diversions, you are actually doing some of the hardest, most courageous work possible. In your quiet, as you stay with it long enough to outwait the internal noises and press into stillness, then, in the silence, you can come face-to-face with yourself, your true self deep within, where you hear and know that you are good, enough, loved, whole, complete, and beautiful. Silence, a benevolent friend, shows us a mirror of who we really are.

In the stillness of your heart and soul, you come into your power, hear your own voice, and know who you are beyond the work identity you wear so well. In quiet, your identity shifts and you know who you are beyond "youth worker, friend, aunt, dad, daughter, employee, author, artist, _____." You shrug off the chains of misidentity that say, "I am only a person if I keep doing, perfecting, pleasing, performing." And you find the confidence and certainty that in your "being," you are so much more than your mere "doing." In silence, you can begin to "reconnect soul and role," as author Parker Palmer says. Sitting with silence lets you shift through the noise of all the demands to a place where you can hear your inner voice and know what is true. It lets you find yourself again.

It is a long journey from a predisposed identification with roles and what people expect to knowing that "you are enough." But it is a worthwhile journey, perhaps the only true journey there is. Poet E. E. Cummings said, "To be nobody but yourself in a world that's doing its best to make you somebody else, is to fight the hardest battle you are ever going to fight . . . never stop fighting."

More Than

It's easy to define your self-concept by the roles you play in life, but you are so much more than that. Is there a role or relationship that you have allowed to dominate your definition of self (spouse, mom, son, builder, teacher, youth worker)? Imagine that you lose that role or relationship; what then? Who are you beneath your "doing" role?

Journal Exercise

Martha O'Brien, a teacher who coaches people on how to do the work necessary to befriend silence and solitude, suggests these practical ideas:

Find a quiet space or create a space in your home that you designate as "the" space. It can be a favorite chair in a room that you enjoy with lots of light. It can be a space you create that serves as a focal point decorated with a candle or objects from nature such as rocks, acorns, and fresh flowers.

Be in that space. Spend five minutes a day, once a day, in your quiet space to start. Work up to twenty minutes a day, preferably in the morning before you get into your whirlwind day.

Journal. Journaling is a way to be quiet with your thoughts. It is a way to get them out and clear the clutter from your head. Journaling can be joyful and offers insights and hope in addition to helping you work out your fears.

Power Truth 4:
Get Outside

Besides making the time to befriend silence, O'Brien also suggests that you broaden your perspective and recognize how vitally connected you are to the world around you. Take time to be in nature. Nature has a powerful healing effect that can be experienced over and over again with no expectations of return payment. It can remind you that you are connected to something much larger than yourself and your concerns. It can show you, season by season, how everything in nature flows with the changes without overt effort and worry—all is well and just as it should be. Nature can reveal the aliveness and the freedom of just being. If you listen, nature is teaching you how to simply be yourself. Be quiet in nature. Observe life around you. Listen to what's going on. Slow down enough to see how active nature is around you and yet how it moves at a steady, unhurried pace. As you cultivate silence outside, you realize just how grand and vast the world is and that you are part of something greater. This realization helps bring a sense of stability and grounding to your day.

Take a Minute

This truth is also important for young people. Youth worker Allison Hurst says, "One student shared with me that sometimes she just really needs 'me time' and 'her own space.' I told her I could appreciate that. So now, if she needs that time, she is allowed to back away from the group and take a minute for herself. I guess I'm just learning that students, like me, find it hard to be 'on' and 'engaged' 100 percent of the time. Sometimes we all just need a short refresher."

Take mindful walks in nature. This will help you stay more present to the moment and the fullness it holds. Be aware of the very act of walking. Feel how the foot grounds itself to the earth. Pay attention to your legs and what they feel like. Note the wind on your face. Observe your breath—is it shallow? Rapid? Deep? Breathe in the smells. And by all means, look up! Quit narrowing your perspective and view by staring at the road just beneath your feet! That creates tunnel vision. Look at the sky and notice its vastness. Think about its vastness to gain perspective. What is nature saying to you? What does the season outside have to say about life? Observe, listen, and engage with nature. Mother Nature has much wisdom to share on the art of being.

Power Truth 5:
Enjoy Life and Play

Give yourself space to enjoy a full life. Play. Read. Create. Build. Ski. Yodel. Hum. Kayak. Dance. Weave. Cook. Bake. Jog. Sing. Garden. Assemble. Draw. Write. Fish. Hunt. Boat. Act. Paint. Run. Photograph. Sew. Farm. Collect. Swim. Climb. Snorkel. Golf. Fence. Shop. Fix. Repair. Bike.

Do: Jigsaws. Crosswords. Sudoku. Board games. Ceramics. Martial arts.

Sports. Radio. Television. Woodworking. Collages. Scrapbooks. Game nights. Finger painting. Ballet. Drag racing. Bungee jumping. Square dancing. Street dancing. Hip-hop. Experiments. Labs. Legos. Pottery.

Create "me" time! Whatever your bliss is, follow it and build time in to connect with the activities and people who fuel your spirit and charge you up! Time spent doing what we love can revitalize us like nothing else. Perspective comes from breaks, whether five minutes, several days, or several weeks. Use this Power Truth to enlarge your life and your heart.

Start Living into Your Power

You *can* live your life from your own power base. It just takes incorporating the untapped Power Truths into your life as part of your daily disciplines. Remember to do the practices of slowing down to notice and pay attention to what's going on in your head and heart, to rest, to clearly know your values, to recharge, to play, to be still, and to remind yourself that you're connected to something much larger than yourself. All these practices aid you in being your best self and maintaining your power.

The key to benefiting from these Power Truths is to just start doing them. Begin. Start. Don't wait for the perfect time or place; just start.

Leo Babauta, in his blog article "The Four Habits that Form Habits," suggests four easy steps anyone can follow to start building new habits. We applied his strategies to self-care in the following ways.

Start small. Exceedingly small. The goal is to create a base of success, so set small goals and then build on them. Like Martha O'Brien said earlier, start with five minutes of quiet or even less. The length doesn't matter. The doing and the achieving do. So if you need to set aside two minutes or one minute each day to be quiet, start there. If it means one minute a day to fit in doing the crosswords (your bliss!), then take that minute. And don't feel guilty! Feel good about taking moments for your own recharging. Doing the habit is the important thing, so let go of that notion that you have to have an hour or it's no good.

Be mindful of negative thoughts. Negative self-talk creeps in often without us even realizing it. We rationalize, dismiss, or give up based on what's going on in our heads. Learn to watch your thoughts and then let them go. They are just thoughts. Stick with your plan for what you intend to do.

Savor the habit. Savor every aspect of what you are doing on your pathway to a more powerful, centered life. Feel it. Feel how good it feels to play. Feel how nice it is to sit and be. Pay attention and enjoy what is going on in your new habit. "Learn to enjoy the habit, and the habit will become its own reward," says Babauta. And that is, after all, the whole point: You living from your best self and doing the things that help you be that person. As you savor the good feelings, you'll begin to look forward to the next time and may even want to spend more time there!

Have a plan for when you falter. Whether that is having someone hold you accountable or giving yourself grace each time to start again, having a plan in place can help you form the base for living out the habits you want to be part of your life.

All of these strategies aim at equipping you to do and be *your very best self.* For you to help youth be their best, you have to do the same. Why? Because you are just as worthy as they are. You matter. You and your youth deserve joy and fullness and to live complete, whole lives.

No Excuses

Think even one minute is too much? That's okay. Start even smaller. If the goal is to start working out at the gym, picture yourself actually lifting weights. Want to meditate? Close your eyes. Take a deep breath. Just start. The act of starting is the "work before the work." It's the mental tuning where you begin the habit of beginning. No excuses. Begin.

Author Marianne Williamson wrote, "Our deepest fear is not that we are inadequate. Our deepest fear is that we are powerful beyond measure. . . . We ask ourselves, Who am I to be brilliant, gorgeous, talented, and fabulous? Actually, who are you not to be? . . . As we are liberated from our own fear, our presence automatically liberates others."

We hope you will not only activate and help youth find their strengths and power but that you will walk in your own power as well.

Keepers. . . . .

What do you want to remember from this chapter? What might you use or try? Flip back through the chapter and skim for possibilities or keepers. Record the ideas that intrigue you, seem possible, or make you excited.

Closing

Every job is a self-portrait of the person who does it. Autograph your work with excellence.

—Unknown

This entire book has focused on building strength in youth and in those who love them. We have sought to provide strategies and tools to help you and your youth gain a sense of self and purpose, develop positive attitudes and outlooks, think critically, be challenged, work together, accept each other, communicate well, and tap into power to contribute to society from a place of passion and giftedness. Hopefully you've collected nuggets that you are excited to implement to help bolster youth from their strengths and build their power.

We want to leave you with the most important thing for you to remember and do: *love*. The most powerful way you can impact youth is by loving them well. Love the young people you work with for who they are and who they will become. Love them enough to get to know them and to let them know you. Love them enough to engage them in activities that they love and in the ways that they like to learn. Love youth enough to set a high standard for them in all areas of life. Love them enough to listen to what they love. Love them enough to help them find ways to explore possibilities and discover sparks, interests, and purpose. Love them enough to step back and let them walk in their own power and strength. Speak loudly of your love for them—and speak often. Love them enough to tell them to slow down and rest. Love young people, and you will see them grow, because love leaves nothing unchanged. It changes everything.

We send well wishes to you as you continue this journey of helping young people be the best they can be. We hope you'll keep in touch with us and share the best practices that are working well for you.

Index . . . .

Acknowledgments . . . .

As is typical for any writing project we undertake, we've collected wisdom from as many practitioners as possible because we admire your work and want to share your experiences. And we've reached out to other authors we admire who graciously agreed to let us reference their works. We hope you, too, will become fans of the brilliant research and strategies of Howard Gardner, John Medina, Gary Smalley, Gary Chapman, Andrew Newberg, and Mark Robert Waldman as you read snippets about their work.

This particular book was definitely a community effort. Thank you *all* for sharing your tips, wisdom, and stories. With the juggling of many ideas, research tidbits, and stories, there is a chance a mistake might have been made in keeping things straight. If so, please forgive us. We are all human— including us authors.

To Anderson Williams and Kelli Walker-Jones, thank you for passionately sharing your philosophies and best practices with us. You, over all others, asked us all the right questions to think more deeply and drew out nuances (from within us) to hold up to the light and let them shine brightly. This book is better because of you.

To our "book world" community, which grew with the writing of this book to include new friends; to everyone who gave of their time for interviews and shared their stories with us—we are grateful you shared your expertise and experiences. It's a joy and comfort to know you are actively engaging with youth. And we are thankful for the opportunity to forge new friendships and deepen existing ones. You humble us.

To the Search Institute team, we are ever so grateful for your belief in us and for partnering with us to empower youth and adults. Some books are tougher than others. Becky Post, you pushed us to share what we know and what we do daily. Karen Chernyaev, you are an editor extraordinaire with an eagle eye who asked us sharp questions. Thank you both for helping birth this book!

To the youth in our lives: You inspire us daily with your energy, heart, and enthusiasm for life. Thank you for filling our lives with joy and hope.

About the Authors ·

Susan Ragsdale and **Ann Saylor** are nationally recognized trainers and best-selling authors of several books. Between them they have more than 40 years of experience in connecting youth with adults and opportunities to grow and develop purpose. Cofounders of the YMCA Center for Asset Development, they have worked face-to-face with more than 12,000 youth and adults since the center's inception, empowering them to live authentic lives of character, service, and leadership. They have reached thousands more people through their seven books, their blog, and their free newsletter. Their mantra "play, live, lead with purpose" is evident in all they do.

Susan is a creativity and reading buff who lives in Nashville with her husband, Pete, and their two feisty, playful dogs, Lacy and Summer.

Ann and her husband, Dan, enjoy sports, reading, playing games, and serving together with their three children in Pleasant View, Tennessee.

Let's Connect More! . . . .

See our books, workshops, blog, and educational resources at
www.theassetedge.net.
Bring us to your city to teach about positive youth development and
building youth power.
Chat with us via Twitter @theassetedge.
Email us at cad@theassetedge.net.

Other Books by Ragsdale and Saylor

Great Group Games: 175 Boredom-Busting, Zero-Prep Team Builders for All Ages

Building Character from the Start:
    201 Activities to Foster Creativity, Literacy, and Play in K–3

Great Group Games for Kids: 150 Meaningful Activities for Any Setting

Get Things Going: 85 Asset-Building Activities for Workshops, Presentations, and Meetings

Great Group Games on the Go: 50 Favorite Team Builders

Ready to Go Service Projects: 140 Ways for Youth Groups to Lend a Hand